*David*

T0270183

# 111 Places
# in the Scottish Highlands
# That You
# Shouldn't Miss

emons:

For my dad, who loved Scotland

**Bibliographical information of the Deutsche Nationalbibliothek**
The Deutsche Nationalbibliothek lists this publication in
the Deutsche Nationalbibliografie; detailed bibliographical data
are available on the internet at http://dnb.d-nb.de.

© Emons Verlag GmbH
All rights reserved
© Photographs by David Taylor
© Cover icon: shutterstock / Shaiith
Layout: Eva Kraskes, based on a design
by Lübbeke | Naumann | Thoben
Maps: altancicek.design, www.altancicek.de
Basic cartographical information from Openstreetmap,
© OpenStreetMap-Mitwirkende, OdbL
Edited by: Rosalind Horton
Printing and binding: Grafisches Centrum Cuno, Calbe
Printed in Germany 2024
ISBN 978-3-7408-2064-0
First edition

*Guidebooks for Locals & Experienced Travellers*
Join us in uncovering new places around the world at
www.111places.com

# Foreword

Wild at heart and abundantly beautiful, the Scottish Highlands is a truly special corner of the British Isles. My first real experience of the region was on a photography trip just over two decades ago. I was enchanted by the landscape then and have remained so on every subsequent visit. I still get a thrill of excitement when standing at the foot of Buachaille Etive Mòr, or watching the sun set over a beach in Assynt. That appreciation has deepened by my learning something of the history of the area, a flavour of which I hope I've conveyed in this book (the human story of the Highlands is fascinating and often heartbreaking).

Wherever possible I've included the Gaelic versions of place names or common words. Pronouncing Gaelic is a challenge for English speakers, however. Take the expression '*slàinte mhath*', for instance, which is Gaelic for 'good health' and is said when raising a glass in company. This friendly phrase is pronounced 'slanj-a-va' and *not* 'slaint muhath', despite how it looks on the page. You won't need to speak Gaelic to make yourself understood in the Highlands, but learning and using a few useful words (hello, goodbye, thank you…) will be appreciated by locals.

Choosing what to include in this book was a tricky (but fun!) problem. Geologically, the Highlands is the area of Scotland north of the Highland Boundary Fault. This ancient dividing line runs diagonally north-east from the Isle of Arran across to Stonehaven on the Aberdeenshire coast. Look at a map. That's a big area! Some of the places in this book are well known and really had to be included. How could Ben Nevis, the highest mountain in the British Isles, be missed out? However, there are other places in this book that are slightly more obscure. They were added in because I really like them and wanted others to experience them too. I hope you enjoy this book and exploring the Scottish Highlands for yourself.

# 111 Places

# 1 Birnam Oak
*The Scottish Play*

There is a unique tree in a strip of woodland near Dunkeld on the southern side of the River Tay. The Birnam Oak is the last of the trees that once made up the more extensive Birnam Wood, a medieval forest with a pivotal role in Shakespeare's *Macbeth*.

Mac Bethad mac Findláich, better known as Macbeth, was a king of Scotland. He began his reign in 1040 after killing Duncan I in a battle near Elgin. Macbeth was king for 17 years until he was killed in battle by Duncan's son, Malcolm (later Malcolm III). By all accounts Macbeth was a wise and just king, who encouraged the spread of Christianity in Scotland.

Shakespeare's Macbeth is far from wise and just. When the play opens, Macbeth is merely one of Duncan's generals. In the company of his ally Banquo, he meets three witches on a 'blasted heath'. The witches tell him that he will one day become King of Scotland, but that it is Banquo's children who will succeed him. Emboldened, and in cahoots with his wife, Macbeth murders Duncan. Macbeth is disconcerted by the prophecy, however. He moves to have Banquo and his son Fleance killed. Banquo is duly despatched but Fleance manages to escape. Macbeth then seeks out the witches and is told that he should beware MacDuff, a local nobleman, but that he 'shall never vanquish'd be until Great Birnam wood to high Dunsinane hill shall come against him'. Reassured, Macbeth has MacDuff's family slaughtered. Grief-stricken, MacDuff persuades Malcolm, Duncan's son, to fight Macbeth. Cunningly using boughs cut from Birnam Wood as a disguise, Malcolm's army defeats Macbeth.

Why did Shakespeare portray Macbeth so negatively? One theory is that it was done to curry favour with James VI, who had recently become King of England. James just happened to be descended from Malcolm III, and so would be more inclined to approve of a play that defamed the reputation of an old enemy of his family.

Address Dunkeld, PH8 0BL, narrates.form.fakes | Getting there Bus 23, 23A, 23C, 23U, 23X, 27 or 27X to Birnam Hotel and then a short walk along Oak Road; just off the B 984 and then on-street parking in Birnam | Tip Birnam Arts is the perfect venue for art lovers, boasting a gallery, artists' workshops, auditorium, shop and café.

# 2 Braemar Gathering
*A living tradition*

How do you test the physical prowess of your nation's men and women without going to war? The modern Olympic Games is a recent solution to that conundrum. Every four years, young athletes from 206 nations compete to win glory for their country. However, the modern Olympics is a relative newcomer. Far older are the Highland Games, held annually in 24 places across the Highlands, as well as in countries such as Australia, Canada and the United States.

Tradition has it that King Malcolm III started the whole thing off in the 11th century. He needed a messenger, and so organised a race to the summit of Creag Choinnich, near Braemar, the winner of which would get the job. The idea caught on. The games became a thrilling way for clans to demonstrate how capable they were, through feats of strength and endurance, as well as through more artistic skills, such as dance and musicianship.

After Culloden, the 1746 Act of Proscription broke the clan system and effectively ended the games. They only returned in 1782, when the act was repealed. One influential fan was Queen Victoria, who had a deep and enduring love of all things Scottish. In 1848, she attended an event at Invercauld organised by the Braemar Highland Society (a 'Royal' prefix was added in 1866). In 1906, the Duke of Fife gifted land to the society to create a permanent arena for what is now known as the Braemar Gathering. (The Duke of Rothesay Highland Games Pavilion is a new addition that houses a fascinating exhibition about the Highland Games.)

Since Victoria, every reigning monarch has attended the Gathering, held on the first Saturday in September. There they, and thousands of visitors, can watch thrilling sports, such as caber tossing and putting the stone, as well as listen to pipe bands and watch deft displays of Highland dancing. There is even a hotly contested hill race, which Malcolm III would surely have approved of.

**Address** Braemar Highland Games Centre, Broombank Terrace, Braemar, AB35 5YX, +44 (0)1339 749220, www.highlandgamescentre.org | **Getting there** Bus 201 to Auchendryne Square and then a short walk; free parking at the centre | **Hours** The Braemar Highland Games Centre is open all year round | **Tip** The ruined Kindrochit Castle in Braemar was built in the 14th century. According to legend, plague broke out inside and so the villagers destroyed it with cannon to stop anyone getting out.

# 3 The Centre of Scotland
*Right in the middle?*

South of Newtonmore, by the side of a quiet single-track road, is a large and conspicuously placed rock. Fixed to the face of the rock is a plaque, on which the words *Centre of Scotland* have been printed in bold type. It's a striking declaration and one that's hard to argue with; somehow it just feels *right*. However, it's an assertion that not everyone would agree with. There are other places in Scotland with an arguably equally valid claim to the title. Is the plaque therefore incorrect? The question is strangely hard to answer definitively, for it all depends on where you measure from.

According to the inscription on the plaque, the stone is *the most distant point from the North Sea and Atlantic Ocean.* However, if sheer distance from a body of salt water is your favoured yardstick, then Glen Quoich (west of Braemar) is the rightful Centre of Scotland. This is the furthest point (just over 42 miles) from the mean high-water mark of the various seas that lap against Scotland's coast, including the country's numerous sea lochs.

Unfortunately for supporters of both claims, the Ordnance Survey has come to a very different conclusion. The OS, rigorously objective to a fault, uses the 'centre of gravity' method to calculate this sort of thing. This imagines Scotland (carefully!) lowered onto the point of a pin. Using this method, the place where Scotland balances (the centre of gravity) is a hill three miles east of Schiehallion. However, this does not take into account Scotland's numerous offshore islands. If you include these (and it's only fair that you should) then the centre of gravity is on the side of a hill east of Loch Garry, within throwing distance of the A9. Despite its proximity to a major road, however, this Centre of Scotland is tricky to get to and hard to find. Happily though, it isn't that far from the Centre of Scotland stone. If you want the strangely satisfying thrill of truly being at the centre of things, that's the place to head to.

Address Glentruim Road, Newtonmore, PH20 1BE, committed.knee.haggling | Getting there Just off the A 86 with limited off-road parking nearby | Tip The adjacent MacPherson Memorial commemorates Ewan MacPherson of Cluny, who led the men of Badenoch on behalf of Bonnie Prince Charlie during the Jacobite rising of 1745.

# 4 The Devil's Elbow
*Turn that steering wheel*

It's all too easy to forget just how good modern cars are. They are reliable, comfortable and safe, with zippy and responsive engines. Features such as anti-lock braking and traction control take the uncertainty out of stopping, and power-assisted steering makes it easy to point a car in the right direction. Driving around the Scottish Highlands today is largely effortless, and rapid progress can usually be made, no matter how steep or twisty the road.

One particularly steep Scottish road is the A 93. Also known as the Cairnwell Pass, the A 93 connects the villages of Blairgowrie and Braemar. Head north from Blairgowrie and you may wonder what all the fuss is about. However, beyond Spittal of Glenshee the road changes character entirely. In just six short miles, the A 93 climbs more than 1,000 feet to attain the giddy altitude of 2,199 feet, the highest point reached by any public road in the United Kingdom. The A 93 achieves this lofty eminence by following a natural valley between Meall Gorm and The Cairnwell, the 3,061-foot peak after which the pass is named.

Look at an Ordnance Survey map of the area and you'll spot a strange feature known as the Devil's Elbow, just a few minutes' drive from the Glenshee Ski Centre and A 93's summit. This is all that's left of an older road, bypassed when the route of the A 93 was subtly altered in the 1970s. The name refers to a notorious double hairpin bend that was reckoned to be Britain's most demanding stretch of road. Signs warned intrepid motorists to proceed with '*GREAT CAUTION*', and passengers on coaches were known to get out and walk rather than take any risks. One driver who was up to the challenge was Prince Philip. A wonderful archive photo shows the prince driving Queen Elizabeth II to Balmoral around the Devil's Elbow. The Queen, regal and obviously unflappable, elected to remain in the passenger seat.

**Address** The Devil's Elbow Viewpoint, Blairgowrie, PH10 7QQ, reporting.lightbulb.jugs | **Getting there** Free parking at the viewpoint and then a 10-minute walk | **Tip** Buy a warming drink and a bite to eat at The Shee Café in the Glenshee Ski Centre.

# 5 Fortingall

*It had to be yew*

Jeanne Calment was 122 years of age when she died in Arles in 1997. During her lifetime, Thomas Edison invented the phonograph, Crick and Watson discovered the structure of DNA, and the Internet was created; *Huckleberry Finn* was first published, so too were the Sherlock Holmes stories, *Animal Farm*, and *Bridget Jones's Diary*; World Wars I and II were fought, as were the Korean, Vietnam and Cold Wars. Calment experienced France's *fin de siècle* period first-hand and almost saw out the second millennium. In short, she lived for a very long time. For a human that is.

There are a number of animal species with lifespans greater than *Homo sapiens*. Jonathan, a Seychelles giant tortoise, celebrated his 191st birthday in November 2023. Hanako, a Japanese koi, was 226 when she died in 1977. And Greenland sharks are thought to be capable of living for nearly 500 years. However, if it's real longevity you seek then you need to be a tree, specifically a yew. Although there is some uncertainty, the Fortingall Yew is thought to be 5,000 or so years old and may well be Europe's oldest tree. If that age estimate is correct, then the yew was already 500 years old when the Great Pyramid of Giza was completed, and approaching 2,000 years of age when Claudius claimed Britain for the Roman Empire.

Although still healthy, time has taken its toll on the tree. In 1769, in a letter to the *Philosophical Transactions of the Royal Society of London*, Daines Barrington stated that he had 'measured the circumference of this yew twice, and therefore cannot be mistaken, when I inform you that it amounted to fifty-two feet'. Daines then noted that 'Nothing scarcely now remains but the outward bark, which hath been separated by the centre of the tree's decaying within these twenty years. What still appears, however, is thirty-four feet in circumference.' The Fortingall Yew is now protected by a stone wall, so it should celebrate many more birthdays yet.

Address Fortingall, Aberfeldy, PH15 2NQ, driver.headers.replaces | Getting there Just off the B 846 with on-street parking nearby | Tip The nearby Cairn of the Dead (Càrn na Marbh) is a Bronze Age standing stone repurposed in the 14th century to mark the burial place of plague victims.

# 6 Grantown-on-Spey
*Town planning, 18th-century style*

Post-war Britain saw the planning and building of what were termed New Towns. These were usually entirely new communities, built from the ground up to either replace old and worn-out housing or to allevi-ate overcrowding elsewhere. Cumbernauld near Glasgow is one such New Town, as is Livingston in West Lothian. However, the concept of creating a town from scratch is far from new. Grantown-on-Spey, at the northern end of the Cairngorms, is a very handsome example of an 18th-century 'New Town'.

It was Sir James Grant of Grant, 8th Baronet, who had the idea of establishing the town. Grant was born in 1738 and was educated at Westminster School. After a university education at Christ's College, Cambridge, Grant embarked on a 'Grand Tour of Europe', during which he collected works of art. According to *The Chiefs of Grant*, published in 1883, he had 'a love of art, and also a kind heart and liberal hand towards rising artists'.

This thoughtfulness was reflected later in life when he took over the running of Castle Grant and its land. Letters written by Grant show 'how anxious he was that good cultivation of land, after the best models, should prevail on the Grant estates'. It was in 1766 that Grantown was founded, with lots marked out 'upon a barren heath moor'. Grant expended the (then enormous) sum of £5000 to 'pro-mote the growth and welfare of the place' so that local artisans and tradesmen provided they were 'of good character' could make a good living there, and provide for their families.

Grant died in 1811 at the age of 73. His death was 'considered as a calamity to Strathspey, and his funeral, the largest ever seen in that country, was attended by miles of mourners, all testifying their devoted attachment to the chief whom they loved so dearly'. For many years afterwards he was referred to in Strathspey as 'good Sir James'. Which is as fond an epitaph as anyone could wish for.

Address The Square, Grantown-on-Spey, PH26 3HG, www.grantownonline.com | Getting there Bus 36A, 37, 37A, 136, 337, 364 or X37 to The Square; just off the A 95 with free car park on Burnfield Avenue | Tip The Grantown Museum is filled with artefacts that tell the story of Grantown-on-Spey and the surrounding area, as well as a rolling series of exhibitions and events.

# 7 — Highlands Wildlife
*Animal magic*

The Scottish Highlands are the place to go to see animals that are either rare or never seen in other parts of Britain. Some of these species are iconic and are indelibly associated with the region.

The largest and most striking species is the red deer. A male (stag) can weigh up to 370 pounds and stand over four feet tall at the shoulder. The most impressive aspect of a stag is his antlers. These are shed in late winter, and a new set grown from spring onwards. Antlers are used during the autumn rutting season to scent mark vegetation, as well as to spar with other males to ensure access to females (does). Deer are found in woodland, as well as open moorland.

Another key species is the golden eagle. These magnificent birds of prey typically have a wingspan of six to seven feet. Though rare, they can be seen flying high over remote glens and upland forests. Their prey is rabbits, hares and birds such as grouse. However, not every large bird in the sky is an eagle. Although buzzards are a far smaller bird, they are regularly mistaken for golden eagles. Buzzards are known a touch dismissively as 'tourist eagles' for this reason. The white-tailed or sea eagle is a cousin of the golden eagle and is found on the west coast of Scotland, particularly the island of Skye.

If you're very lucky you may see a beaver in the Highlands. This is not an animal that immediately leaps to mind when thinking of Scottish wildlife. There is a sad irony to this, as beavers were once widespread across the whole of Britain. By the early 16th century, the entire British beaver population had been hunted to extinction for its fur and scent glands. The latter produces a substance called castoreum, which is used in traditional medicine, in perfumery, and is also said to enhance raspberry and strawberry flavourings in ice cream. In May 2009, European beavers were reintroduced to Scotland, in Knapdale Forest. The success of this scheme has resulted in similar projects elsewhere in Scotland.

**Address** One place to see wildlife is the Mar Lodge Estate National Nature Reserve, Braemar, Aberdeenshire, AB35 5YJ, +44 (0)1339 720163, www.nts.org.uk, chips.caked.mealtime | **Getting there** Follow the unclassified road from the A 93; free parking at Inverey Car Park (annotated.trying.many) or paid parking at the Linn of Dee Car Park (digested.scan.impeached) | **Hours** Open all year round | **Tip** The Grant Arms Hotel is known as the 'Wildlife Hotel' for its rolling programme of wildlife-themed events and short breaks.

# 8 Laggan
*Adapted for the screen*

Compton Mackenzie was born in County Durham in 1883 to an English father and American mother, but he was a Highlander by both descent and inclination. He was a truly prolific writer, writing nearly 100 books on a wide variety of subjects. Two of his best-loved novels are set in his spiritual home: *Whisky Galore* and *The Monarch of the Glen* (the title of a painting by Sir Edwin Landseer).

*Whisky Galore* relates the wartime exploits of the inhabitants of the (fictional) island of Great Todday, who 'rescue' hundreds of cases of whisky from the wreck of the cargo ship SS *Cabinet Minister* just before she sinks. The islanders' attempts to keep this treasure out of the hands of excise men, as well as away from the pompous Paul Waggett, captain of the island's Home Guard unit, drives the amusing plot. The novel was adapted as a feature-length movie by Ealing Studios in 1949, which features a young Gordon Jackson.

Published in 1941, *The Monarch of the Glen* is also wonderfully funny. The story is set in the (fictional) Scottish castle of Glenbogle. Chester Royde, an American millionaire, is staying in Glenbogle with his new wife Carrie, who has Scottish ancestry, and sister Myrtle. They are guests of the eccentric chief of Clan MacDonald, Donald MacDonald. During their stay, the National Union of Hikers, under the leadership of the prim Sydney Prew, are discovered trespassing on the laird's estate, and disturbing the grouse. MacDonald vows to defeat the unwanted incomers, and somehow marry one of his sons off to the eligible Myrtle too.

In 2000, the BBC (very) loosely adapted *The Monarch of the Glen* for television. In this version, Archie, son of Hector and Molly, is tricked into returning to Glenbogle, only to discover that the estate is facing financial ruin. Ardverikie House, near Loch Laggan, stood in for Glenbogle, and a variety of locations in the charming hamlet of Laggan were used to represent the Glenbogle estate village.

**Address** Laggan, Newtonmore, PH20 1AH | Getting there Bus 140 to Bridge and then a short walk; free parking in the village just off the A 86 | Tip Take a tour round the Dalwhinnie Distillery and taste a selection of their renowned single malt whiskies.

# 9 Lecht Mine
*Any old iron*

It's hard to believe, but now-quiet corners of the Cairngorms once rang with the sounds of industry. One such place is Lecht Mine on the Glenlivet estate. The first mine at the site was sunk in 1730 by the York Buildings Company to extract iron ore. As there was no wood for a furnace at Lecht, the ore was transported 20 miles to Nethy Bridge for smelting. The resulting ingots of iron were known as 'Stradoun Pigs', Stradoun being an old name for Strathavon. Transporting the ore was an expensive and time-consuming business that required 120 heavily laden ponies. Ultimately, the mine proved to be uneconomical and closed in 1737.

Charles Gordon-Lennox, 5th Duke of Richmond, decided to have another go in 1841. This time round, the product was manganese – often found in close proximity to iron ore. Manganese is a hard but brittle metal that has a number of uses, such as acting as a catalyst during the production of bleach. It's also added to steel to increase the tensile strength of the alloy, as well as to improve its resistance to wear. Steel was an important resource in mid 19th-century Britain, so it's easy to see how Gordon-Lennox thought that reopening an old mine might be a canny financial investment. The signs were initially promising. Lecht Mine still holds the record as the largest manganese mine ever operated in Scotland, and at one point employed over 60 men and boys. Unfortunately, cheap Russian imports depressed the need for domestically mined manganese. Lecht Mine closed for the second and final time in 1846.

The most visible trace of the mine is the austere but handsome two-storey crushing mill. A (long-gone) waterwheel drove rollers and hammers that smashed the manganese ore into a powder, which was transported to Buckie, and from there on to Newcastle upon Tyne by boat. Happily, recognising its importance, Moray Council restored the mill in 1983. It is now a listed building.

Address The Old Military Road / A 939, Tomintoul, AB37 9ES, welcome.scoping.science | Getting there Free parking in a small car park off the A 939 and then a 20-minute walk along a grass path | Tip Look out for the Well of Lecht on the walk to the mine building. This is a white stone plaque erected in 1754 to commemorate the building of the Old Military Road by the five companies of the 33rd Regiment.

# 10 __ Old Packhorse Bridge
*Crossing the River Dulnain*

The Bridge of Carr or the Old Packhorse Bridge in Carrbridge strad-dles the River Dulnain. It was proposed on 23 May, 1717 by Brigadier-General Sir Alexander Grant, Laird of Grant, and built later that year by mason John Niccelsone (or Nickolson) from Ballindaloch. It is thought to be the oldest stone bridge still standing in Scotland, though it is semi-ruined and no longer in use.

The Dulnain is a fast-flowing river and in full spate is impossible to ford, so the specification stated that the bridge should be of 'ane reasonable Breadth and Height as will Receive the water when in the greatest speat'. The total cost of construction was £100, which was partly paid for using a stipend from the parish of nearby Duthil. At the time, Duthil had no minister, so parishioners could use the 'vacant stipends' for 'pious uses'. The bridge quickly became known locally as 'the coffin bridge' as it was used as a route to Duthil Church by funeral processions. It was also used by foot travellers and horse riders, as well as farmstock.

A neighbouring bridge was built in 1791, initially to carry the Kin-veachy to Dulsie Bridge military road. Carrbridge owes its existence to this bridge. The first building erected nearby was an inn (now the Carrbridge Hotel), with the village gradually following on afterwards. This second bridge is long gone, replaced by a modern and, it has to be said, slightly dull road bridge.

The Old Packhorse Bridge looks the way it does now due to dam-age sustained in the 'Muckle Spate' of 3 August, 1829. In *An Account of the Great Floods of August 1829 in the Province of Moray and Adjoining Districts* (1830), the bridge was said to be 'a picturesque object, but the flood has rendered it still more so, by entirely removing the remains of its wing-walls, and leaving its tall, round-shaped, skele-ton arch, standing thin and meagre-like'. It's in this depleted but still charming state that you can see it today.

Address B 9153, Carrbridge, PH23 3AL | Getting there Bus 37, 136 or X 37 to Artists Studio; train to Carrbridge and then a 15-minute walk; on-street parking on Station Road and then a short walk | Tip The Landmark Forest Adventure Park is a fun amusement park with something to entertain every member of the family, from life-sized animatronic dinosaurs to a tropical butterfly house.

# 11 Prince Albert's Pyramid
*Four-sided tribute*

Prince Albert of Saxe-Coburg and Gotha was the great love of Queen Victoria's life. The match was artfully arranged by King Leopold I of Belgium, who was uncle to them both. They first met on (the then Princess) Victoria's 17th birthday in April 1836. Victoria was very taken with Albert and he with her. In her diary, Victoria wrote that 'he is extremely handsome; his hair is about the same colour as mine; his eyes are large & blue & he has a beautiful nose & a very sweet mouth with fine teeth'. However, in 1837, before marriage could be considered, Victoria became queen. This complicated things somewhat, prompting the question of who should propose to whom. The matter was settled in October 1839 when Victoria popped the question. On 10 February, 1840, the couple were married in the Chapel Royal, St James' Palace.

Unfortunately, although it was a happy marriage, it was destined to be short. Albert died of what was thought to be typhoid fever on 14 December, 1861, aged just 42. (It's now believed that he may have expired from abdominal cancer as he'd suffered from stomach cramps since 1859.) Victoria did not take the untimely death of her husband well. For the rest of her life she remained in mourning, wearing black no matter what the occasion. She also insisted that Albert's rooms in their various houses be maintained, even to the extent of having the bedclothes and towels changed daily.

A more monumental tribute to Albert is a granite pyramid commissioned by Victoria and built in the grounds of her Balmoral estate. An inscription on the cairn reads: *To the beloved memory of ALBERT, the great and good Prince Consort. Erected by his broken-hearted widow VICTORIA. R. – 21st August, 1862.* Unlike a pharaoh, however, Prince Albert wasn't interred inside. His mortal remains were placed in the Royal Mausoleum, Frogmore, where Victoria eventually joined him after her death in 1901.

Address Balmoral, Ballater, AB35 5TL, +44 (0)13397 42534, www.balmoralcastle.com, shows.thigh.ultra | Getting there Bus 201 to Balmoral Road End and then a (steep) 40-minute walk following 'The Great Pyramid of Scotland' route; take the A93 to Crathie and then paid parking at the Balmoral / Crathie Car Park, from where you follow the Pyramid route | Hours Open all year round | Tip The grounds and gardens of Balmoral Castle are open during the spring and summer months (see website for details).

# 12 Ruthven Barracks
*Hanover vs Stuart*

The reign of King George I could so easily have come to a quick and ignominious end. George was born in Germany in the city of Hanover and barely spoke English when, in 1714 at the age of 54, he was crowned King of Great Britain and Ireland. He got the job as his great grandfather was King James VI of Scotland (later James I of England), and because he was Protestant. Another contender was the exiled James Stuart, son of King James II who was deposed during the Glorious Revolution of 1688. However, James was Catholic and barred from the throne after the 1701 Act of Settlement.

Supporters of James and his claim to the throne were known as Jacobites, after *Jacobus*, Latin for James. In September 1715 the Jacobites struck. Led by the Earl of Mar, they captured Inverness, Aberdeen and Dundee. By early October, Mar and his army held all of Scotland north of the Firth of Forth. However, Mar was oddly indecisive during a number of battles, never quite pressing home the advantage he had over the often-outnumbered Hanoverian armies. Gradually, the Jacobites ceded ground. On 22 October, the Jacobites lost the Battle of Preston, Lancashire, ending the uprising and any hope that James could become king.

The end of the Jacobite Rebellion did not mean the end of unrest in Scotland. And so, in 1719, Ruthven Barracks was built to house British government troops. They were stationed there to enforce the 1716 Disarming Act. This was a law that attempted to secure 'the peace of the Highlands in Scotland' by outlawing Highlanders from having 'in his or their custody, use, or bear, broad sword or target, poignard, whinger, or durk, side pistol, gun, or other warlike weapon' without authorisation. Ironically, the barracks are now in a ruinous state because the act was unsuccessful. In 1745, the Jacobites rose again, this time in support of Charles Stuart, son of James. On 17 April, 1746, the Jacobites destroyed the barracks.

Address Kingussie, Newtonmore, PH21 1NR, www.historicenvironment.scot, thirsty.
probably.denim | Getting there Bus 39, 138, 139, 140 or M 39 to the Duke Of Gordon
Hotel and then a 20-minute walk; train to Kingussie and then a 15-minute walk; just off the
B 970 with free parking opposite the Ruthven Barracks site | Hours Open all year round |
Tip The Iona Gallery is run by the Society of Badenoch and Strathspey Artists to showcase
the varied work of its members, all of whom live in the Cairngorms National Park.

# 13__ Schiehallion
*Massively attractive*

In the summer of 1774, Astronomer Royal, Nevil Maskelyne, in the company of Charles Hutton and surveyor Reuben Burrow, stood on the slopes of Schiehallion with a pendulum. The men were there to measure the mean density of the Earth, a task funded by the Royal Society. The iconic Perthshire mountain was thought to be the ideal place to achieve this goal.

Schiehallion is strikingly symmetrical along its east to west axis. From Loch Rannoch, thanks to perspective, the mountain looks conical and uncannily like a volcano. It also stands alone, with no other large peaks in its immediate vicinity. Maskelyne believed that a pendulum would be deflected from its default vertical position by the gravitational attraction of a mountain. After much searching, Schiehallion was chosen precisely because of its unusual symmetry and isolated position. It was thought that by measuring how far the pendulum was deflected it would be possible to work out the density of the mountain, and ultimately of the Earth itself.

To provide a fixed reference point, the team of scientists first made observations of the stars from both the north and south slopes of Schiehallion (the ruins of the purpose-built observatories can still be seen today). This process took some time, due to the Scottish weather. Eventually, however, after the observations were complete, the experiment proper was finally able to get under way.

It took until 1776 to complete all of the required measurements. Hutton was then tasked with performing the complex calculations necessary to provide a figure for the Earth's density. (One useful by-product of Hutton's work was the invention of contour lines, which are still used to neatly convey the shape of hills and mountains on maps today.) Hutton's eventual figure of 5.3 billion trillion tons was only 20 per cent less than the modern figure of 6.6 billion trillion tons, a truly remarkable achievement for the time.

**Address** Pitlochry, PH16 5QE, push.embodied.alley | **Getting there** Paid parking at the Braes of Foss Car Park just off the Schiehallion Road (vines.chickens.breeze) and then a two to three-hour walk to the summit (depending on fitness levels and weather conditions) | **Tip** The interesting Old Church of Rannoch in Kinloch Rannoch was built in 1829 by Scottish civil engineer Thomas Telford.

# 14__Shinty
*Scotland's national sport?*

Largely unknown south of the border, the Scottish sport of shinty has a loyal and enthusiastic following in its native country – particularly in the Highlands. There is a four-tier shinty league administered by the Camanachd Association, and newspapers and local radio regularly report on matches.

Shinty is played between 2 teams of 12 men or 10 women on a grass field with a goal at either end. A game lasts 90 minutes, split into two halves of 45 minutes. Each team member has a two-sided wooden stick – known as a caman – that is used to play the (hard but surprisingly small) leather ball. The ball can be dribbled along the field with the caman, or lofted elsewhere to a fellow team member. The ball can also be played in the air, which is how a shinty match begins: the referee throws the ball up between two opposing players who use their camans to try to gain control of the ball. Unlike hockey, players can use their chests to play the ball, and can stop the ball by using both feet together.

The aim of shinty is to score more goals than the opposing team. To stop someone from scoring, an opposing player can use their caman to either block the ball or take control of it. Players can also make shoulder-to-shoulder contact to put their opponents off their stride. What players *cannot* do is swing their caman into that of an opponent. This is considered to be a foul, with the victim awarded a free hit from the spot where the foul took place. Dangerous play can result in a player being shown a yellow warning card or, if the transgression is particularly bad, a red card. At that point, the player will be sent off the pitch and their team will be down one member.

A great place to learn more about the sport is at the Highland Folk Museum in Newtonmore. There you can visit a 1930s shinty pavilion. And, in the summer months, you may also catch a game of shinty being played on the neighbouring field.

Address Highland Folk Museum, Newtonmore, PH20 1AY, +44 (0)1349 781650,
www.highlifehighland.com | Getting there Bus 39, 139 or M 39 to The Balavil Hotel
and then a short walk; take the Highland Folk Museum turn-off on the A 86 and park
at the museum (fee payable) | Hours Daily Apr–end Aug 10am–5pm, Sep–end Oct
10.30am–4pm | Tip See a variety of exotic animals at the Highland Wildlife Park,
including tigers, bison and Arctic foxes.

# 15 Wildcat Trail
*Miaow*

Any cat – even the most placid and pampered puss – is apt to turn into an angry ball of fur should a meal or two be unforthcoming. However, no matter how mad the mutinous moggy may be, the Scottish wildcat can trump it when it comes to bad attitude.

Britain's last native cat species, the Scottish wildcat (*Felis silvestris*) does look vaguely similar to the family feline. Their grey-brown striped coat resembles that of a domestic tabby – hence the nickname of 'Highland tiger' – but they are stockier, and have a larger flatter head and a bushy tail, ringed with a black tip. They are also more burly and sport longer legs than a typical house cat.

Unlike civilised kitties, the Scottish wildcat has to catch its own food. This is usually small rodents, such as voles and rabbits, but can also include birds, fish and lizards. They are most active at dawn and dusk, when they use their superb hearing and vision to track down and catch their prey. Despite their fierce appearance, Scottish wildcats are incredibly shy. You're more likely to see signs that they're around – paw prints or scat – than the creatures themselves.

Unfortunately, the Scottish wildcat is on the critically endangered list. They were once relatively common across the whole of Britain. Now their range has shrunk to the central Scottish Highlands, which includes the Cairngorms, the Black Isle, Aberdeenshire, and the Angus Glens. This decline has largely been through persecution by farmers and gamekeepers, who saw them as vermin, as well as hybridisation with domestic cats. There are conservation efforts underway, but time is sadly not on the wildcats' side.

If you want to find out more about the Scottish Wildcat, then The Wildcat Centre in Newtonmore is for you. There are also over 130 individually decorated models of wildcat scattered in obvious, and not so obvious, places around the town. You can even claim a prize should you manage to spot them all.

Address Main Street, Newtonmore, PH20 1DD, +44 (0)1540 673131, www.wildcatcentre.org | Getting there Bus 39, 139 or 140 to Monarch County Apartments; take the B 9150 from the A 9 and park at the free car park on Glen Road | Hours The Wildcat Centre is open Fri–Mon 10am–4pm | Tip The Clan Macpherson Museum tells the story of the clan, one of whom was Ewan, a Jacobite who evaded capture for nine years after the Battle of Culloden before escaping to France.

# 16 Duncansby Stacks

*Temporary (geologically speaking)*

Caithness is blessed with a number of impressive coastal features, arguably the finest of which are the Duncansby Stacks. A sea stack is a vertical tower of rock, formed when the sea and weather (wind and rain, as well as frost) gradually erode a gap in a coastal cliff. (A sea arch such as Needle Eye Rock is essentially just a sea stack that hasn't quite detached itself from its cliff.) The process of erosion is relentless, however. Eventually, the base of the stack is worn away too, causing the stack to collapse into the sea. This is unlikely to happen with the Duncansby Stacks any time soon, though this will be their eventual fate.

The two main stacks at Duncansby are sharply triangular and jut out of the sea like the teeth of a giant carnivorous creature. The unusual pointed structure was caused by the weather whittling away the upper section more quickly than the sea shaped the base. The stacks are thought to have separated from the cliff roughly 6,000 years ago. However, the sandstone from which they are formed is some 390 million years old, the end result of sand and mud from ancient lakes building up in thick layers over millennia.

Duncansby Stacks may not have survived the 1950s had the British military got their way. Although it's hard to believe now, a scheme in early 1953 to detonate an atom bomb on top of one of the stacks was seriously considered. Caithness is relatively underpopulated, and it was thought that testing a nuclear device there wouldn't be *too* disruptive. The bomb would have been similar in size to a fridge freezer and would have exploded with the force of 16,000 tons of TNT. Ultimately, it was wet weather that saved the stacks, as it was thought that the damp climate would affect the device's electronic firing system (which unsurprisingly was felt to be *far* from ideal). The bomb was finally tested in the far drier climate of South Australia later that year.

**Address** Duncansby Head, Wick, KW1 4YS, pizza.exacted.homelands | **Getting there**
Bus 80, 280 or 913 and then an hour's walk; take the Duncansby Head road from the A 99,
park for free at Duncansby Head Lighthouse Car Park and then a 20-minute walk | **Tip** The
Duncansby Head Lighthouse was built after World War I to help ships navigate through
the treacherous waters of the Pentland Firth.

# 17 Dunnet Head
*'Lots of planets have a north'*

There are many truly singular things to see and do in the Scottish Highlands. You could take yourself to the top of the highest mountain in the British Isles (Ben Nevis, of course); visit the deepest lake (Loch Morar, home to a monster called Morag); or have a wee dram in the most remote pub in Britain (the Old Forge in the village of Inverie, the largest settlement in Britain not connected to the road network). Dunnet Head (Ceann Dùnaid) offers a unique experience too. This wild spit of land on the Caithness coast is the northernmost point on mainland Britain. You cannot get any further north in the UK without hopping on a ferry.

Unlike the better-known and more popular John O' Groats, Dunnet Head lacks facilities. There are no gift shops, hotels or even loos. There is, however, a wonderfully austere Victorian lighthouse, built by Robert Stevenson (grandfather of novelist Robert Louis Stevenson). The lighthouse is still in use but closed to visitors (it has been fully automated since 1989, when the last lightkeeping family moved out). More accessible are the five buildings and infrastructure of a World War II naval radar station. The station started operating in December 1940 and was built to detect German U-Boats and shipping sailing through the Pentland Firth, as well as keeping a look out for enemy aircraft that just happened to be lurking in the area.

A good chunk of the Dunnet Head peninsula is now managed by the RSPB. During the spring and summer breeding season, the cliffs of Dunnet Head are home to hundreds of thousands of sea birds, such as fulmars, kittiwakes, guillemots, razorbills and puffins. The cliff-top viewing platform is the best spot from which to watch their comings-and-goings. You can often see seals too, sunning themselves on the rocks below the cliffs. If you're very lucky you may even see pods of dolphins or killer whales out at sea.

Address B 855, Dunnet, Caithness, KW14 8YE, +44 (0)1463 715000, www.rspb.org.uk, overheard.hardens.brownish | Getting there Take the B 855 from the A 836 and then park at Dunnet Head | Tip Castletown Heritage Centre is a great place to discover more about the social history of the area, as well as the tradition of creating flagstones from local stone.

# 18   Ebenezer Place

*Blink, but don't miss it*

It doesn't take long for Wick's postie to deliver mail to Ebenezer Place, for it is a mere six feet nine inches long and boasts just one doorway. The singular entrance leads to the No 1 Bistro, which belongs to Mackay's Hotel around the corner on Union Street. In 2006, Ebenezer Place was listed in the *Guinness Book of Records* as the shortest street in the world. This honour came after a visit to Wick by editor-in-chief, Craig Glenday, to confirm the record. Glenday 'battled through gale-force winds and storms' to get to Wick, but it took him less than an hour to reach his decision. The then owner of Mackay's, Murray Lamont, was delighted, stating at the time that 'it has certainly become a great point of interest'.

Mackay's Hotel is a wedge-shaped building with Ebenezer Place at the narrow end of the wedge. It was built in 1883 by Alexander Sinclair, a wealthy Scot who had recently returned from the United States. Bizarrely, the town council decided that the end of the building should be designated as a street in its own right, despite the slender aspect. And so, in 1886, Ebenezer Place first appeared in the town's records. No one now knows why the name Ebenezer was chosen, though there may be a masonic connection.

Until 2006, the shortest street in the world (according to Guinness) was the 17-foot-long Elgin Street in Bacup, Lancashire. However, a more contentious claim on the record has been made for McKinley Street in Bellefontaine, Ohio. This street is – depending on how you measure it – between 15 and 30 feet long. Although longer than Ebenezer Place and (possibly) Elgin Street too, McKinley Street does have a road attached, which makes it a proper street according to local supporters. That Ebenezer Place was finally recognised in 2006 was all down to Lamont, who first thought to invite the man from Guinness northwards. Mackay's Hotel has benefited from the unique claim ever since.

**Address** Ebenezer Place, Wick, Caithness, KW1 5ED, +44 (0)1955 602323, www.mackayshotel.co.uk | Getting there Bus 82, 99, 276, 282, 917, 918 or X99 to Caithness General Hospital; train to Wick; follow the A99 to Wick and park at Victoria Place | Tip The Castle of Old Wick is a ruined medieval castle on a narrow promontory overlooking the North Sea.

# 19 John O' Groats
### *The end or the beginning?*

John O'Groats isn't the most northerly point of the British mainland, nor is it the most northerly settlement (those would be Dunnet Head and Scarsferry, respectively). John O'Groats is, however, a must-see location near the very top of Scotland, and one that hundreds of thousands of excited tourists flock to every year. One draw is the famous fingerpost on which are displayed the distances (in miles) to places in the British Isles and beyond.

The town was founded in the reign of King James IV of Scotland by Malcolm, Gavin and (the eponymous) Jan de Groot, who between them built a house near where the modern hotel stands. A low mound now marks the spot. According to *The Statistical Accounts of Scotland (volume VIII)* of 1793, the three were 'supposed to have been brothers, and originally from Holland'. They were in possession of 'a letter written in Latin, by that prince [James], recommending them to the countenance and protection of his loving subjects, in the county of Caithness'. For many years, Jan de Groot ran a ferry service to Orkney. After his death, he was buried in the churchyard of Canisbay Kirk, the most northerly church on the mainland and just a few miles west of John O'Groats. A memorial stone in the vestibule of the church commemorates his life.

John O'Groats is often twinned with Land's End in Cornwall, some 603 miles away (as the crow flies). Numerous charities have benefited financially from people making their way from Land's End to John O'Groats (or vice versa). Generous folk have sponsored attempts to walk the distance, to cycle between the two, or drive a combine harvester from one to the other (a feat achieved by Olly Harrison and his team, raising £35,000 for Mind and Children with Cancer in the summer of 2023). Perhaps the oddest effort was that of Stephen Gough, who walked the 900-mile route *sans* clothes to express his 'human right' to be naked in public.

Address John O'Groats, Caithness, KW1 4YR | Getting there Bus 80, 280 or 915 to Car Park; train to Wick; take the A 99 from Wick and park at John O'Groats Car and Coach Park (parking charges apply) | Tip Orkney (specifically South Ronaldsay) is just a 40-minute ferry ride from John O'Groats.

# 20   Latheronwheel Fairy Glen
*Would suit (very) small family*

If you go down to the woods today, you may get a big surprise. There may not be teddy bears lurking in Latheronwheel Glen but it *is* where fairies live. Don't believe me? Then you'll just have to go there yourself and see if you can spot one. You'll have to be as quiet as a mouse though, for fairies have excellent hearing and are very, very shy. Not many people can creep along quietly enough to catch a fairy unawares…

Even if you don't spot one, you can see their wonderfully sweet houses nestled in the undergrowth (don't knock on the doors though, as the fairies won't answer). Rather cleverly, the fairies have made good use of old tree stumps and mossy rocks to build their homes. After all, why buy bricks and concrete when you can use what Mother Nature has left behind? Even though they dwell deep in a wood, the fairies live a comfortable life. One fairy has made a playground for the fairy children (isn't that thoughtful?). And a friendly fairy has laid a picnic table ready for visitors. Perhaps there *are* teddy bears in the woods after all…

Just like you and me, fairies have hobbies and interests. One fairy would rather be a pirate – wouldn't you be one if you could? Another owns a little rowing boat – perhaps he or she likes to sail out to sea on adventures. There's a fairy who lives in a caravan, and another who owns a wishing well (what do you think fairies would wish for?). One fairy makes ladybirds welcome, as everyone should. And guess what the fairy who lives at 'Fishermen's Rest' does with his day? He's not a boring accountant, that's for sure.

Some naughty folk (adults and big brothers and sisters) will tell you that it's not the fairies who made the houses. They'll state as fact that it's local volunteers who do the work. Don't listen to them. They were wrong about Santa Claus, and they're wrong about this. Fairies do exist and they live in Latheronwheel Fairy Glen.

**Address** Latheronwheel, Caithness, KW5 6DR, saved.slick.dude | **Getting there** Bus 99, 918 or X 99 to Bus Shelter and then a short walk; take the Latheronwheel turn-off from the A 9, park at Latheronwheel Harbour and then a short walk | **Tip** The Buldoo Stone near Latheron is a 12-foot-tall, 5,000-year-old menhir erected during the Neolithic or New Stone Age.

# 21 Needle Eye Rock
*For the birds*

Needle Eye Rock is a dramatic 150-foot-tall sea arch on the east coast of Caithness. It is arguably *the* most dramatic sea arch in Scotland – possibly even in the British Isles! – and yet curiously is not widely known about. This may be to do with its relative remoteness and inaccessibility, as it can only be viewed either from a boat or by peering over the side of a *very* high and vertiginous sea cliff. (Don't get *too* close to the edge…) Also known as Wick Sea Arch, the more descriptive moniker is sensibly thought to derive from the way the shape of the arch resembles the eye of a needle.

It *is* worth a visit, despite the effort it takes to get there, particularly during the summer months when the cliffs are crowded out with nesting sea birds. One species commonly seen perched on the narrow rock ledges is the common guillemot. This handsome chocolate-brown bird is a member of the auk family, which also includes razorbill and puffin (both of which can be seen on the Caithness coast too, the latter at Puffin Cove near Drumhollistan). Guillemots don't make nests, which allows them to congregate in huge numbers on cliffs, often just inches away from each other. This makes their eggs and chicks less likely to be snatched by predatory birds such as gulls. Female guillemots only lay one egg a year, which is pyriform, or pear-shaped. This makes the egg less prone to rolling off the edge than a more rounded egg.

Another commonly seen species is the kittiwake, a member of the gull family. Their name derives from their distinctive call of 'kitti-wa-aaake'. Like guillemots, kittiwakes congregate on cliff ledges to protect their eggs and chicks, though they are the only gull to nest *exclusively* on cliffs. Sensibly, kittiwake chicks don't wander too far from their nest, preferring to sit still until ready to fledge. Kittiwakes spend the winter months out at sea, so once the breeding season is over you won't see them again until the following year.

Address Near Corbiegoe, KW1 5TU, chambers.homeward.fatherly | Getting there Take the Sarclet turn-off from the A 9, park at Sarclet Harbour and then follow the John O' Groats Trail northwards for the 30-minute walk to the Needle Eye Rock viewpoint | Tip Sarclet Harbour was used to land herring between the 18th and early 20th centuries.

# 22 Nucleus
*The mighty power of the atom*

The starkly modern Nucleus facility does duty as a repository for the records of Britain's nuclear industry, as well as providing a home for the historical archives of Caithness. The latter consists of a wide variety of documents from the 15th century onwards, and includes maps, photographs and family records, as well as official papers such as charters and minute books. If you want to research your Caithness family history – or just have a hankering to learn more about the area generally – then Nucleus is *the* place to visit.

Ultimately, Nucleus will store all of the records relating to the civilian nuclear power plants built and operated by the United Kingdom Atomic Energy Authority. There are so many documents and files that the transfer will take a number of years to complete. The oldest records date back to the late 1940s, when Britain first began to experiment with nuclear reactors to generate electricity. That, and to (secretly) provide a source of fissile material – such as plutonium – for use in British atomic weapons.

The first large scale nuclear power station connected to the National Grid was Calder Hall in Cumbria in 1956, now better known as Sellafield. Two Scottish nuclear power stations were also commissioned during the 1950s: Hunterston A in Ayrshire, and Dounreay on the northern coast of Caithness. Electricity first flowed into the grid from Dounreay's Fast Reactor on 14 October, 1969. A second reactor – a Prototype Fast Reactor or PFR – began to supply power in early 1975.

Nothing lasts forever, though. Dounreay no longer generates electricity: the original reactor was shut down in 1977, followed by the PFR in 1994. Dounreay is now being dismantled with a view to reusing the site for other purposes. Unfortunately, the complexity of the process, and the decontamination required, means that this may take until the year 2333.

Address Wick Airport, Wick, Caithness, KW1 4QS, +44 (0)1955 602444,
www.highlifehighland.com | Getting there Bus 80, 82, 99, 276, 282, 917 or X 99 to Hill
Avenue and then a 10-minute walk; take the Wick Airport turn-off from the A 99 and park
at Nucleus | Hours Mon–Fri 9am–5pm (booking ahead to view the Caithness archives is
recommended) | Tip Dounreay Nuclear Power Station can be seen (at a distance) from an
official viewing platform just off the A 836.

# 23__Nybster Broch
*Home from home*

A broch is a uniquely northern Scottish Iron Age structure. They were huge circular stone towers some 40 feet high with walls up to 16 feet thick, topped off by a thatched roof. Remarkably, they were built using a dry-stone wall technique without mortar or cement to hold them together. It was once believed that brochs were simply the fortified strongholds of local chieftains – the word broch derives from 'brough', the Lowland Scots for fort. Thanks to modern excavations of various brochs, it's now thought that they were actually (very sturdy) domestic dwellings. It's also entirely possible that they served both purposes at different times.

The best-preserved example of a broch is found on the island of Mousa in Shetland. At 44 feet high, this largely intact broch still provides an excellent view west across Mousa Sound to the mainland. The brochs of Caithness and Sutherland are far less complete, though still fascinating. Nybster Broch, first excavated by Sir Francis Tress Barry in 1895, is a typical example. It stands on a promontory on the east coast of Caithness. Although the remaining stonework is barely above waist height, the basic round shape of the tower is still visible. The foundations of external buildings can also be seen arrayed around the perimeter of the tower, and show that Nybster Broch was at the heart of a small village.

An excavation in 2011 revealed that Nybster Broch was occupied between 1,500 B.C. and A.D. 500, although it was modified and remodelled several times over this lengthy span of time. Animal bones from horses, sheep or goats, cattle and pigs, as well as dogs, cats and rabbits were also found during the dig. The abundance of cattle and sheep bones is evidence that these animals were important to the inhabitants of Nybster Broch, both for milk and wool, as well as for meat. The bones of mice and rats were also found, so unwelcome house guests were a problem 2,000 years ago too.

Address Nybster, Wick, KW1 4XP, www.thebrochproject.co.uk, feasted.stoppage.assure |
Getting there Free parking at Nybster Broch Car Park just off the A 99 and then a short
walk | Tip Keiss and Whitegate Brochs are curiously close together, raising further questions
about the original purpose of brochs.

# 24  Old Pulteney Distillery
*Briefly surplus to requirements*

For most people in Britain, 28 May has very little significance, unless it happens to be Spring Bank Holiday. However, for those who live in Wick, this particular date marks the beginning of a curious social experiment. For it was on 28 May, 1922 that the sale of alcohol was comprehensively banned in the town.

Remarkably, prohibition was self-inflicted. By the early 1920s, Wick was one of Europe's largest herring fishing ports. The influx of workers to catch and process the fish had led to a sharp increase in Wick's population over the 19th and early 20th centuries. Unfortunately, the newcomers liked a dram or two after work, behaviour that was frowned upon by the more upstanding and religious inhabitants of the town. The passing of the 1913 Temperance (Scotland) Act allowed local councils to prohibit the sale of alcohol if a majority of voters were in favour of a ban. Supporters of temperance got their way when 62 per cent of the town voted for prohibition. Presumably to the dismay of the other 38 per cent, pubs were summarily closed, and hotels in Wick could no longer legally serve drinks to guests (no matter how much they pleaded).

All of this put Wick's Old Pulteney Distillery in an invidious position. By 1922, Old Pulteney had been making whisky for 96 years. Now it could no longer sell its product locally, or in other Scottish towns, such as Kirkintilloch and Lerwick, which had imposed similar bans. Despite a fall in sales, the distillery managed to hold on until 1930 when it finally closed for business.

Wick's prohibition lasted exactly 25 years, ending on 28 May, 1947. The Temperance (Scotland) Act remained on the statute books until it was replaced by the Licensing (Scotland) Act in 1976. The Old Pulteney Distillery made a spirited return in 1951 under its new owner, Robert 'Bertie' Cummings. It has been making its highly regarded single malt whisky ever since.

**Address** Huddart Street, Wick, Caithness, KW1 5BA, +44 (0)1955 602371, www.oldpulteney.com | **Getting there** Bus 276 or 914 to Council Yard; train to Wick and then a short walk; follow the A 99 to Wick and either park at Victoria Place or find on-street parking nearby | **Hours** Apr–Sep, Mon–Sat 10am–5pm; Oct–Mar, Mon–Fri 10am–4.30pm (see website for information on tours and prices) | **Tip** Castle Sinclair Girnigoe, near Wick, is an atmospheric ruin on a *very* vertiginous cliff overlooking the sea.

# 25 Reay Cross Slab
*Ancient wonder*

Hidden inside a nondescript one-storey building in a churchyard in the village of Reay is a cross delicately carved in stone. This is truly a case of a lamp hiding under a bushel, for this is an artistic and architectural marvel. The Reay Cross is a Pictish Christian relic dating back at least 1,000 years, if not a few centuries more.

The building in which the cross stands is the Old Parish Church of Reay, originally dedicated to St Colman. The church was probably built in the 16th century, long after the cross was sculpted. During the 1700s, the cross was out in the churchyard and being put to use as a grave-marker. If you look closely you'll notice that the top stem of the cross is missing its original tracery. This was removed to add the words *Robert Mackay 17* to the cross. The figure probably represented a year of death that was for some reason never completed. This inscription was in turn removed (very crudely) when the cross was moved inside the church in the early 20th century.

The Picts were the descendants of the original inhabitants of Scotland. The term is derived from *Picti*, Latin for 'painted people'. It was first used by the Romans in the 3rd century in reference to the Pictish practice of covering the body with decorative designs. In all likelihood it was also an insult, applied by the invaders to any northern Briton unlucky enough to find himself or herself living in the uncivilised wilds outside the empire's borders.

The Picts were converted to Christianity in the 6th century by St Ninian and St Columba. For nearly 400 years, they created wonderfully ornate carved cross slabs, of which Reay Cross is a splendid example. These slabs feature geometric symbols, such as lines and circles, as well as representations of Scottish animals, such as stags, eagles and salmon. The Picts were also adept at metalwork and jewellery. The Rogart Brooch, on display in the National Museum of Scotland, is a particularly fine example of their craft.

Address Reay, KW14 7RE, roofer.vouch.twitching | Getting there Bus 274, 800, 803 or 921 to School; on-street parking just off the A 836 nearby | Hours Generally accessible 24 hours though the gate is occasionally locked | Tip The distinctive (new) white Reay Parish Church was built in 1739. On the front wall of the church is an iron hook. The hook was once used to punish wrongdoers, who would be attached to the hook by a leather collar and left to face derision from anyone passing by.

# 26 Thurso Railway Station

*The southbound train is now departing*

Britain has an extensive rail network that routinely gets people quickly and efficiently from one place to another. (Your experience may differ...) However, there are some journeys that should not be undertaken lightly. It's fine travelling from one town to the next, but it's not so simple if you want to get from one end of the country to the other. Start from London (King's Cross) and it will take you a minimum of 12 hours and at least three changes of train to finally arrive in Thurso, the northernmost railway station in Britain. It's even worse if you live in Exeter, Swansea, or any other southern city some distance from the East or West Coast Main Lines. You're now looking at a full day's travel, or roughly the time it would take to fly from London to Sydney. Scotrail weren't kidding around when they named the line from Inverness to Thurso the Far North Line.

The line from Inverness to Thurso was built and opened in stages between 1862 and 1874. Designed by Murdoch Patterson, Thurso Railway Station was opened on 28 July, 1874. Two early passengers to Thurso Station were Edward, Prince of Wales, and his wife Alexandra. The royal couple travelled up from Dunrobin on 2 October, 1876. Edward, accompanied by the Duke of Sutherland, rode in the engine cabin for the entire journey. The Duke was a real railway enthusiast and so this must have seemed like a dream come true. The engine driver and his stoker were less enthused however, as the two VIPs proved to be 'a bloody nuisance'.

The Far North Line was threatened with closure in the early 1960s. This came after the British government published *The Reshaping of British Railways*. More popularly known as the 'Beeching Report', the detailed review called for the closing of lines that were deemed unprofitable or underused. This included the entire railway network in northern Scotland. That the Far North Line survived is a welcome miracle.

Address Princes Street, Thurso, KW14 7DL, www.scotrail.co.uk | Getting there Bus 280, 803 or 917 to station; train to Thurso Railway Station; on-street parking nearby | Hours Open during scheduled train timetable hours | Tip The nearby Mill Theatre is owned and run by the Thurso Players, an amateur dramatic society who have been entertaining locals since 1950.

# 27 Whaligoe Steps

## *Herring aid*

Thomas Telford was a man whose opinion mattered. In 1790, he was hired to survey the coast of Caithness by the extravagantly named British Society for Extending the Fisheries and Improving the Sea Coasts of the Kingdom of Great Britain, thankfully otherwise known at the British Fisheries Society. Telford was a civil engineer, and had the expertise to assess which of the county's harbours were suitable for expansion, or decide where new ports could be usefully built. Fishing for herring was a lucrative business and the members of the BFS were keen to capitalise on this.

At some point on his travels, Telford visited Whaligoe, a natural inlet on the eastern coast of Caithness. According to *A Tour in Scotland 1769 (volume one)* by Thomas Pennant, Whaligoe – 'a creek betwixt two high rocks' – was already used to land fish as 'the country people have made steps by which they go up and down, carrying heavy burdens [creels full of fish] on their back; which a stranger, without feeling, would scarcely believe'. Despite the tenacity and ingenuity of the locals, Telford described Whaligoe as a 'dreadful place' and gave it the thumbs down.

Ignoring Telford's conclusion, Captain David Brodie of Hopeville decided to proceed with the task of improving Whaligoe. In 1792, Brodie spent £53 on 'clearing the harbour by blasting and removing large stones and building a platform for boats to secure them from being carried away', as well as £8 for 'making stairs in the face of the rocks to lead down to the boats'. It was money well spent. In 1808, seven herring boats regularly sailed from Whaligoe. By 1855, that number had risen to 35.

The demand for herring gradually declined in the latter half of the 19th century, and Whaligoe ceased to function as a harbour. Brodie's steps were saved for posterity in the 1970s by the heroic Etta Juhle. They are now in the care of local volunteers.

Address Whaligoe, Lybster, KW2 6AB, bitter.troubles.afflicted | Getting there Bus 99, 275, 918 or X 99 to Smithy Cottage and then a short walk; free on-street parking on Watenan Road just off the A 99 near Loch Watenan (recoup.applauded.colonies) and then a 10-minute walk | Tip The nearby Cairn o'Get is the site of a 5,000-year-old chambered burial tomb that would once have been over nine feet high.

# 28__ Wick Heritage Centre
*The silver darlings*

The delightful Wick Heritage Centre is a treasure trove of domestic and industrial artefacts from the town of Wick. It's all too easy to spend all day looking at the exhibits and still not see everything (which is no bad thing as that gives you a great excuse to make a return visit!). The collection is incredibly varied too. Name another museum where you can find a moustache cup, a state-of-the-art washing machine from the 1920s (it's no longer state-of-the-art…), a hard-labour machine from a Caithness jail, and a pair of nursery rhyme fireplace tiles.

Arguably the most fascinating section of the centre is the one dedicated to the history of Wick's herring fishing industry. The story begins in 1767 when three Caithness men, John Anderson, John Sutherland and Alexander Miller, began to fish for herring from Wick. What made their efforts particularly lucrative was a subsidy paid by the British government to owners of herring boats larger than 60 tons, plus an extra bounty for any herring subsequently sold abroad. The example of the three men (Miller became extremely wealthy) led to a boom in herring fishing from Wick.

Herring is an oily fish that rots quickly after being caught unless processed one way or another. Smoking or curing a herring creates a kipper. In the early 20th century, there were 50 smoking kilns in Wick, the largest of which was able to cure 90,000 herring at a time. You can step into a 1940s kiln at the heritage centre and see replica herring hanging from their 'tenterhooks'.

The job of gutting the fish was left to the 'herring lassies'. This was itinerant summer work, with many of the women travelling across from the Hebrides. For three months or so, a 'herring lassie' would spend long days gutting an average of 40 fish per minute on the harbour front. Curiously, many fishermen would not allow the women onto their boats as this was considered bad luck.

Address 18–27 Bank Row, Wick, KW1 5EY, +44 (0)1955 605205, www.wickheritage.org |
Getting there Bus 275 or 282 Lower Dunbar Street and then a short walk; train to Wick
and then a 10-minute walk; on-street parking on Bank Row | Hours Easter–Oct Mon–Fri
10am–5pm, Sat 11am–3pm | Tip Wick's old fog cannon was gifted to the town by Sir John
Pender MP in 1881. It was fired during foggy conditions as a warning signal to seafarers
sailing along the Caithness coast.

# 29___Wolfburn Distillery

*Slàinte mhath!*

It's 1828, you live in Caithness and you fancy a wee dram. Where do you go? An advert in *The Scotsman* would have been timely. A Leith-based trader named George Thomson boasted that he 'continues to receive orders for Thurso Aquavitae, made at Wolfburn Distillery, by Wm. Smith'. The enterprising William Smith had started his distillery in 1821, on a farm a mile west of Thurso. He named his venture after the Wolf Burn, a small stream from which he drew water for the distillery. In 1826, Smith's annual production was 28,056 'Total Gallons of Proof Spirit', and Wolfburn was the largest distillery in Caithness. It also had the unique distinction of being the most northerly distillery on the British mainland.

An advert dated 16 September, 1848 in the *John O'Groat Journal* was more sombre. Under the intriguing title of 'EXCELLENT INVESTMENT', the advert began, 'To be LET in consequence of the decease of the Tenant, for the remainder of the current lease, of which twelve and a half years have yet to run, the well-known DISTILLERY of WOLFBURN, with the good will of the business'. Entrepreneurs tempted by this opportunity were reassured that 'It has been paying well hitherto, and could not fail to pay much better in the hands of enterprising parties.'

Sadly, the distillery barely lasted another decade or so. The exact date of closure is now lost, but an Ordnance Survey map of 1872 shows the distillery 'in ruins'. You can't keep a good idea down, however. In 2011, the Wolfburn name was revived when Aurora Brewing received planning permission to build a new distillery less than 400 yards from the site of the old. Two years later, the first whisky was laid down on 25 January, Burns' Night. The small but passionate team, led by distillery manager Iain Kerr, have since brought acclaim to the Wolfburn name. And it is *still* the furthest north of any distillery on the British mainland.

Address Henderson Park, Thurso, KW14 7XW, +44 (0)1847 891051, www.wolfburn.com | Getting there Bus 274, 275 and various others to Weigh Inn Hotel and then a 10-minute walk; take the Wolfburn Distillery turn-off on the A 836 and then find on-street parking nearby | Hours Weekday tours (see website for details) | Tip Discover the history of Caithness at the North Coast Visitor Centre.

# 30 Clava Cairns
*Round and round we go*

According to an article in the *Inverness Courier* dated 27 September, 1837, the Rev Charles Lesingham Smith 'though the fellow of a College, is a rather light tourist, somewhat garrulous, and neither very profound nor very penetrating'. Happily, the author of the piece also noted that Smith 'appears to be an amiable man, with a taste for scenery'. The article then continued with a long and very detailed description of Clava Cairns, taken from Smith's (then new) book, *A Highland Tour by an English Clergyman*.

Smith described 'the most perfect' of the three cairns as a 'great conical heap of small stones… hemmed in at its base by a circle of larger ones fixed in the ground' and that 'in the midst of the cairn there is a hollow chamber, the walls being formed of layers of loose stones or slabs'. This is as good a description of the cairns now as it was then. Smith didn't get everything right, however. He wrote that the original builders of Clava Cairns were 'barbarous' Scandinavians (did they perhaps transport the cairns over the sea in flat pack form?). We now know that the cairns were constructed by native Scots during the Bronze Age, some 4,000 years ago.

The longer and more formal title of the Prehistoric Burial Cairns of Balnuaran of Clava is a better clue as to the purpose of the site. Each cairn was a chambered tomb built to house the remains of one or two people. Given how much time and effort would have been spent on their construction, the cairns were probably reserved for people of importance, such as a local chief.

Some of the large outer stones of the cairns are decorated with cup and ring marks. The purpose or meaning of these mysterious symbols is long lost; they may have been purely decorative or perhaps had some religious purpose. It's possible that builders of the cairns found the stones elsewhere and essentially recycled them. Perhaps they found the markings an aesthetically pleasing puzzle too.

Address Inverness, IV2 5EU, www.historicenvironment.scot, tour.sparkles.grapevine |
Getting there Signposted from the B 9092; free parking on-site | Tip The Barevan Lifting
Stone near Achindown is a round granite boulder that has traditionally been used as a test
of male strength (don't put your back out trying to lift it though…). It may also have been
used to temporarily trap people in a nearby stone 'coffin' as a form of punishment.

# 31 Culloden Battlefield

*Jacobites vs Redcoats*

Prince Charles Edward Louis John Philip Casimir Sylvester Maria Stuart was the son of the exiled James Stuart, and (thankfully) more commonly referred to as Bonnie Prince Charlie. On Tuesday, 15 April, 1746, Charles arrived with his 6,000-strong Jacobite army at Drummossie Moor near Culloden.

Charles had landed in Scotland the year before with dreams of taking the three crowns of Scotland, England and Ireland from King George II on behalf of the Stuart family. His campaign had successfully taken him and his men as far south as Derby, before the Jacobites' position became untenable. Charles then made his way north again, hoping to wage a decisive battle against George's army on Scottish soil. Ironically, the man in charge of that army, the Duke of Cumberland, was a distant cousin of Charles.

Drummossie Moor was a poor choice for a last stand. Charles' army relied on a tactic known as the 'Highland Charge' to overwhelm the enemy. The flat, boggy moorland would make this ploy far less effective. However, Cumberland's army failed to turn up on the 15th. The Duke and his men were in Nairn, celebrating his 25th birthday. Charles then made the unfortunate decision to march his army to Nairn, hoping to catch Cumberland unawares. They marched through the night, only to fall two miles short of Nairn by daybreak. Realising their mistake, the Jacobites turned around and marched back to Drummossie Moor. Cold, tired and hungry, their spirits must have fallen further when the skirl of bagpipes announced the arrival of Cumberland and his troops.

The ensuing battle was bloody and decisive, and took less than an hour. By the end, over 1,500 Jacobites lay on the battlefield, either dead or close to death. Charles fled, eventually reaching Rome, where he died in 1788. The defeat at Culloden ended the dream of a Stuart once again sitting on the British throne.

THE BATTLE
OF CULLODEN
WAS FOUGHT ON THIS MOOR
16TH APRIL 1746.

THE GRAVES OF THE
GALLANT HIGHLANDERS
WHO FOUGHT FOR
SCOTLAND & PRINCE CHARLIE

**Address** Culloden, Inverness, IV2 5EU, +44 (0)1463 796090, www.nts.org.uk | **Getting there** Bus 27 to Culloden Battlefield; parking at the Visitor Centre | **Hours** Battlefield open daily; Visitor Centre open daily 3 Jan–28 Mar 9am–4pm, 29 Mar–30 Sep 9am–6pm | **Tip** The Prisoners' Stone in Culloden Wood is where 16 Jacobite soldiers are said to have been executed after the Battle of Culloden. The story was related by a seventeenth soldier who survived and managed to escape.

# 32__ The Falls of Foyers
## *Cold water for Burns*

Robert 'Rabbie' Burns was born in South Ayrshire on 25 January, 1759. Known as Burns Night, Scots rightly celebrate this auspicious date with a hearty supper of haggis, neeps and tatties, accompanied by a dram or two of whisky. Burns is granted this singular honour for the simple reason that he is Scotland's national poet. His poems and songs, often written in a light Scots dialect still delight today, and cover such subjects as love and friendship, Scottish history, and nature. On Burns Night, his 'Address to a Haggis' is traditionally read out loud as the eponymous dish is brought to the table, and 'Auld Lang Syne' (sometimes in tune) is sung at the stroke of midnight on 31 December to welcome in the New Year.

Burns was a lowland Scot and lived in southern Scotland all his life. However, in the summer of 1787, he embarked on a near month-long tour of the Highlands. On 5 September, the poet visited the Falls of Foyers. So inspired was he by the sight that he whipped out paper and pencil and immediately 'composed these lines standing on the brink of the hideous caldron below the water-fall'. The resulting 'Lines On The Fall Of Fyers Near Loch-Ness' describes how 'The roaring Fyers pours his mossy floods / Till full he dashes on the rocky mounds', though the view is 'Dim-seen thro' rising mists and ceaseless showers'.

Visit the waterfall today and you've every right to be puzzled by the poem. The falls are impressive, but they are definitely *not* the 'whitening sheet' described by Burns. The blame for this can be laid on Britain's first aluminium smelter, opened in 1896 on the banks of Loch Ness. Water was diverted from the River Foyers along a half-mile-long tunnel to generate electricity for the plant. This had the effect of reducing the falls to a relative trickle. The smelter closed in 1970, though the river is still used to generate electricity. This completely green energy is now fed into the National Grid.

Address Foyers, IV2 6XU, states.dare.boring | Getting there Bus 302 to Upper Foyers Shop and then a short (if steep) walk; just off the B 852 with paid parking at Upper Foyers | Tip Look for Nessie from a roadside viewpoint further north along the eastern shore of Loch Ness on the B 852 / General Wade's Military Road.

# 33 Felicity the Puma

*The big friendly moggy*

It all began in Tomich when, in 1976, Jessie Chisholm claimed to have seen a big black cat. One year later a man and his nephew reported seeing a 'lioness and two cubs' in a field at Farr, just 10 miles from Inverness. And then Donald 'Ted' Noble began to lose sheep from his farm near Cannich. Often all he'd find were the butchered carcasses of his livestock, the bones crushed and chewed. In October 1980, after seeing something worrying his Shetland ponies, Ted set a trap to capture what was obviously a large and fierce creature.

What Ted caught was a puma, a big cat normally found on the continents of North and South America. However, Ted's puma – a female – was oddly tame and unusually plump for a wild animal. A vet who examined the cat believed that she had spent her life in captivity as a pet, and may only have enjoyed freedom for a few weeks or possibly even days. The puma was taken to the Highland Wildlife Park where, given the name Felicity, she spent the rest of her days. Felicity was a popular attraction at the wildlife park and was described as 'very tame indeed' by Eddie Orbell, the Park Director. She particularly enjoyed riding around on the shoulders of her keeper, Donald Mitchell, whose children also played with her. Felicity died of old age in January 1985, peacefully in her sleep. Shortly afterwards she was preserved by a taxidermist and put on display at the Inverness Museum and Art Gallery, her relaxed and affable pose an accurate reflection of her friendly nature when alive.

Attacks on farm animals continued after Felicity was captured, though neither Ted nor anyone else has ever managed to trap another puma. Felicity was too tame to be the original culprit – and she definitely didn't match the description given by Jessie Chisolm. Reports of big cats continue to come in every so often, so keep your eyes peeled when out in the hills near Inverness or you may be in for a big surprise.

**Address** Inverness Museum and Art Gallery, Castle Wynd, Inverness, Highland, IV2 3EB, +44 (0)1349 781730, www.highlifehighland.com | Getting there Bus 7, 14 or 14D to Town House; train to Inverness and then a short walk; paid parking at Castle Street Town House Car Park | Hours Apr–Oct Tue–Sat 10.15am–4.30pm, Nov–Mar Tue–Thu noon–4pm, Fri & Sat 11am–3.45pm | Tip See local wildlife at the Merkinch Local Nature Reserve on the Beauly Firth at the north end of Inverness.

# 34 Leakey's Bookshop
*For bibliophiles*

You need a lot of space for books. If you regularly buy the things (but don't sell them or hand them on to others afterwards) then you'll know how hard it is find room for them all. One bookshelf for your expanding collection soon becomes two, and then three, four, five… Eventually you find yourself looking for a new and far larger house, preferably one with reinforced floors and planning permission for an extension, just in case.

Charles Leakey has faced a similar problem several times in his life. Charles is the eponymous owner and founder of Leakey's Bookshop in Inverness, which opened its doors in June 1979. Charles' second-hand bookshop was run from a first-floor room in Grant's Close, what was then a narrow lane between High Street and Baron Taylor's Street. Charles soon found that these premises were too small, and so he moved his shop to a larger place in 1982. By 1994 it was time to relocate again. The venue Charles chose was the former Greyfriars Free Church on Church Street.

The first church on this site was St Mary's Gaelic Church, built in 1649 for the religious Gaelic speakers of Inverness. The original building was comprehensively altered in 1792, and again in 1822 under the supervision of architect James Smith. The owners of the building sold it to Charles, preferring his proposal to that of someone who planned to open a nightclub in the building.

The modifications Charles made to the building were sympathetic, and included adding an upper floor (reached via a spiral staircase), as well as a large wood-burning stove. Some of the original features can still be seen, of which the most prominent is the original pulpit. There are roughly 100,000 books on sale, though neither Charles nor his son Sam, who helps run the shop, know exactly how many books there actually are. What is known is that Leakey's is now the largest second-hand bookshop in Scotland.

Address Greyfriars Hall, Church Street, Inverness, IV1 1EY, +44 (0)1463 239947, www.leakeysbookshop.com | Getting there Bus 14, 48A, 61, 300A or 421 to Academy Street; train to Inverness and then a short walk; paid parking at Old Town Rose Street Car Park | Hours Mon–Sat 10am–5.30pm | Tip The Highland Archive Centre in Inverness collects and preserves archives that chronicle the history of the Highlands from the 14th century onwards.

# 35 Loch Ness
*Cryptozoology*

Newspapers in 1933 were all a twitter with reports of a strange creature spotted living in Loch Ness. In May that year, *The Aberdeen Press and Journal* reported the 'Loch Ness "Monster" again seen' and that 'people who have come forward with the most authentic stories speak of a "monster" between twenty and thirty feet long with a body like that of a huge overgrown eel'. Readers were assured that 'Mr Alex. Gray, a bus driver, who resides at Foyers, is to make an attempt to catch it', the resourceful Mr Gray having had 'special tackle made'. The *Daily Mirror* quoted Sir Murdoch MacDonald, MP for Inverness, who said 'Nobody knows what is there, but it is quite obvious that too many people have seen something for the matter to be ignored.'

The following year the *Daily Mail* published what is now known at the 'Surgeon's Photograph'. The snap taken by Robert Kenneth Wilson showed what looked to be a long-necked creature poking its head out of the water. It caused a sensation and sparked an interest in the Loch Ness Monster that has hardly abated since.

In 1972, a scientific team led by Robert Rines shot two grainy underwater images of what seemed to be a flipper, similar in shape to the limbs of a plesiosaur, an extinct sea-dwelling reptile that lived during the time of the dinosaurs. This led Rines and naturalist Peter Scott (son of Antarctic explorer Robert Falcon Scott) to propose a Latin name for the creature: *Nessiteras rhombopteryx*. Their case was undermined when Scottish MP Nicholas Fairbairn pointed out that this was an anagram of 'Monster hoax by Sir Peter S'. (Rines quickly countered with 'Yes, both pix are monsters R.').

The 'Surgeon's Photograph' was revealed to be a hoax in 1994; 'Nessie' was probably a shaped piece of wood mounted on a model submarine. So, is the Loch Ness Monster just a figment of the imagination, or is it real? No one knows. But the truth is out there.

**Address** Explore Loch Ness from Fort Augustus or Drumnadrochit | **Getting there** Bus 919 to Medical Centre (Fort Augustus) or 312, 917 or 919 to Borlum Farm (Drumnadrochit); paid parking in both towns | **Tip** Take a cruise along Loch Ness with Loch Ness by Jacobite – seeing Nessie is sadly *not* guaranteed.

# 36 The Malt Room
## *The Water of Life*

Who invented whisky? The Scots, of course. Or was it the Irish? Or possibly an influential 9th-century chemist from Iran. The latter was Abū Mūsā Jābir ibn Ḥayyān, who invented the alembic pot still and experimented with the distillation of alcohol.

Jabir's writings on the subject eventually found their way to the monasteries of western Europe. The alcohol produced by monks following Jabir's example was primarily used for its medicinal qualities, to treat diseases such as smallpox and palsy. It was in a Scottish (or Irish) monastery that someone had the bright idea of fermenting cereal grain mash, the main ingredient still used to make modern whisky (barley being the grain of choice in Scotland).

The Irish *Annals of Clonmacnoise* gloomily notes that 'Richard or Risdard maGranell, chieftaine of Moyntir-eolas, died at Christmas [1405] by takeing a surfeit of *aqua vitae*, to him *aqua mortis*. 'This is the first written record referring to *aqua vitae*, Latin for 'water of life'. In (Scots) Gaelic *aqua vitae* is *uisge beatha*, which, after some tinkering to suit English speakers, became the word whisky.

The Scottish government saw an opportunity to increase its tax revenue once whisky became a commercial product; the first excise duty on whisky was applied in 1644. This led (unsurprisingly) to widespread illicit distillation of whisky across Scotland. Modern commercial production essentially dates to 1823, when the Excise Act was passed. This allowed the distillation of whisky for an annual licence fee of £10, and a payment of 2/3d per gallon of proof spirit. George Smith was one of the first to apply for a licence. Glenlivet, the distillery he founded, continues to produce whisky today.

The perfect venue to try a dram or two is the Malt Room in Inverness. Owner Matt McPherson is a spirited advocate for whisky, and has created an atmospheric setting in which to begin your journey into the wonderfully varied world of whisky.

**Address** 34 Church Street, Inverness, IV1 1EH, +44 (0)1463 221888, www.themaltroom.co.uk | Getting there Bus 5, 5C, 6 or 8 to Queensgate (Stop A); train to Inverness and then a short walk; paid parking at Old Town Rose Street Car Park and then a short walk | Hours Mon–Sat noon–midnight, Sun 3pm–midnight | Tip Take a tour round Uile-bheist Distillery at the southern end of Inverness.

# 37__NC500

*Follow the signs*

Scotland's Highland coast is truly spectacular and wonderfully accessible. The North Coast 500 – or NC500 – is a 516-mile road route cunningly devised to tempt more people to experience the northern coast. The route starts (and ends) at Inverness Castle. When driven anti-clockwise, you follow the Caithness coast north to John O'Groats. From there you strike westward for Durness, before taking the winding road south to Applecross. After that it's a (still beautiful) cross-country drive back to Inverness.

The NC500 was launched in March 2015 by the North Highland Initiative. At the time, the NHI chairman, David Whiteford, stated that the creation of the NC500 was 'an opportunity to create a globally significant route that captures the essence of the wonderful landscapes and seascapes, people, stories, culture, history, adventures, food and drink and much more'.

The NC500 hasn't been immune to criticism, however. It's a route to be savoured and not rushed. And yet there are those who want to complete the run in the shortest amount of time possible. This is potentially dangerous, particularly along the windy single-lane sections. Encouraging the use of motor cars is also questionable. In an interview for *The Scotsman*, outdoor writer and broadcaster Cameron McNeish made the point that 'for a country whose government is so concerned with renewable energy and climate change is it not hypocritical for its tourism body to support such a way of seeing Scotland?' The increase of traffic on formerly quiet roads has contributed to the increasing deterioration of those roads too.

Despite these problems, there is no denying that the NC500 is a world-class route. It was no surprise to anyone that *Condé Nast Traveller* described the NC500 as 'the ultimate UK road trip', or that CNN (rightfully) declared that 'the route boasts some of the most dramatic scenery in Europe'.

Address Inverness Castle, Inverness, IV2 3EG, www.northcoast500.com, hosts.late.plus | Getting there Bus 4 or 14A to Castle Street; train to Inverness and then a short walk; by car take the A 82 to Inverness and park at Rainings Stairs Car Park (fee payable) | Tip Inverness Castle is also the start (or end) of the Great Glen Way, a 79-mile walking route between Inverness and Fort William.

# 38 Shooglie Bridge
*Wibbly-wobbly*

The pedestrian London Millennium Bridge opened to great fanfare on 10 June, 2000. Unfortunately, it quickly suffered from 'synchronous lateral excitation' as people walked across it. In other words, it wobbled. On 12 June, the bridge was shut for two years while extensive (and successful) modifications were made to the structure. Since 2002 the bridge has served London well and is a useful link between Bankside and the City of London. Despite this, the bridge is still referred to as the 'wobbly bridge'.

Shooglie (or shoogly) is the wonderfully mellifluous Scottish word that means to wobble, sway or shake about. Like London, Inverness has a pedestrian bridge that wobbles, but unlike Londoners, the good people of Inverness are rightfully proud of their shooglie crossing. The Greig Street Bridge is a three-span suspension footbridge across the River Ness that links Greig Street on the west bank and Bank Street on the east. It was built in 1880 at a cost of £1,400 by C. R. Manners, who practised as a civil engineer and architect between 1875 and 1909. The iron to build the bridge was provided by the nearby Rose Street Foundry, owned by the Northern Agricultural Implement and Foundry Company Limited. The foundry is long gone as is the company, though the firm's handsome head office on Academy Street has been recently restored.

The Greig Street Bridge doesn't wobble all the time; it takes a concerted effort and a gang of like-minded people to create the effect. The key is persuading the group to walk roughly a third of the way across and then have them jump up and down in unison. This creates a vertical sine wave-like movement along the length of the bridge, which is very disconcerting for anyone unaware of what's going on. Although the experience is open to anyone with enough friends, it's typically young folk who like to cause the bridge to bounce, or rather shoogle like a jelly.

Address Inverness Castle, Inverness, IV2 3EG, vocal.stream.bossy | Getting there Bus 4 or 14A to Castle Street; train to Inverness and then a short walk; paid parking at Rainings Stairs Car Park | Tip Far larger (and less shooglie) is the Kessock Bridge, which carries the A9 over the Beauly Firth, and from which you can view Inverness to the south and the Moray Firth to the north.

# 39 St Columba's Well
### *A saint helps out*

In A.D. 563, Columba travelled to Scotland from his native Ireland with 12 followers. Columba was a Christian missionary who had already founded a number of churches and monasteries in Ireland. He was now determined to bring Christianity to the Scots and Picts. To this end, he and his companions first established a monastery on the island of Iona in the Inner Hebrides.

Columba has a number of connections to Loch Ness. The most famous is an encounter with the Loch Ness Monster, thought to be the first ever recorded. According to the legend, Columba asked a monk to swim across the loch and return with a boat moored on the other side. The unlucky disciple was halfway across when Nessie reared up out of the water and, with a great roar, sped towards the poor man. Thinking quickly, Columba cried out 'Go no further, nor touch the man! Go back!' This the creature did, leaving the swimmer unharmed, though presumably somewhat shaken by the experience.

Another helpful act attributed to Columba occurred around 565, when the monk was travelling through the Great Glen on a mission to convert Brude, leader of the Picts, to Christianity. *En route* to Brude's court in Inverness, Columba took the time to found a church in Invermoriston. He was also called on to bless a well, the waters of which were said to cause painful boils and blisters when touched. This Columba did, making the water safe to drink from that day on.

Columba died on Iona in 597, and was buried in the monastery he founded. The Celtic Church later canonised him by acclamation, and he is regarded as one of the Twelve Apostles of Ireland. Iona is still a place of pilgrimage, though Columba's remains were moved off Iona after Vikings raided the island in the 9th century. Fittingly, his relics were split between Ireland and Scotland.

Address Inverness, IV63 7YA, positives.copying.pitch | Getting there Bus 312 or 917 to Hotel; free parking at Invermoriston Falls Car Park | Tip Urquart Castle, one of the largest castles in Scotland, sits dramatically on a small headland that juts out into Loch Ness. The castle is now a romantic ruin, having suffered repeated raids in the 16th century and a Jacobite siege in 1690.

# 40__ Town House
*PM puts holiday on pause*

The Town House has the unique distinction of being the first (and, until 2008, the only) place in which the British Cabinet has met outside London or Chequers. This was the result of a crisis in Ireland.

In 1541, after centuries of warfare and attempted conquest by England, King Henry VIII had himself crowned King of Ireland. What followed was the subjugation of Ireland's largely Catholic population. One form this took was the settling of Protestant English and Scottish landowners in the northern counties of Ireland, collectively known as Ulster. On 1 January, 1801, Ireland was formally joined to the United Kingdom following an Act of Union. However, calls for Irish Home Rule intensified throughout the 19th century. Independence came close in September 1914 after the Government of Ireland Act was passed. Unfortunately, the new war in Europe saw the act suspended for the duration.

In 1916, the Irish took action. The Easter Rising that year led to the Proclamation of the Irish Republic. However, the rebellion was harshly put down by the British, inflaming the situation further. In December 1918, the republican Sinn Féin party, under the leadership of Éamon de Valera, won three-quarters of Irish parliamentary seats following a general election. Refusing to sit in Westminster, de Valera convened the Dáil Éireann in Dublin instead.

What followed was the Anglo-Irish War, which rumbled on until a truce was negotiated in July 1921. There were still problems to resolve, however, including that of Ulster. That summer, the British PM, David Lloyd George, was on holiday in Gairloch, and (coincidentally) other cabinet members were on holiday in Scotland too. Rather than return to London to discuss the matter, Lloyd George summoned the cabinet to the Town House instead. The meeting on 7 September resulted in the 'Inverness Formula' and ultimately to the treaty that created the Irish Free State in 1922.

Address Castle Street / High Street, Inverness, IV1 1JJ | Getting there Bus 7, 14 or 14D to Town House; train to Inverness and then a short walk; paid parking at Castle Street Town House Car Park | Hours Visible from the outside only except during occasional pre-booked tours arranged through the Inverness Museum and Art Gallery (www.highlifehighland.com) | Tip Blackfriars Burial Ground is the site of a medieval friary, founded in 1233. The only remnant of the friary is a single stone column in the burial ground.

# 41 Victorian Market
*A phoenix from the ashes*

The elegant, covered Victorian Market in Inverness houses a wonderfully eclectic range of independent shops and cafés. It opened to great fanfare at noon on 25 May, 1870. The following day, the *Inverness Courier* reported that 'the frontage to Academy Street is tastefully designed, and the space inside is fitted up in a suitable manner with stalls and tables' and that 'its general appearance is very compact and commodious'.

Disaster struck the market on 23 June, 1889 when a fire broke out in the early morning. According to the *Courier*, this was 'the most destructive fire which has occurred in Inverness during the last forty years'. Because of its wooden construction, the market was 'soon enveloped in flames, which spread to the rear of the shops and the roofs of the houses in Union Street'. Unfortunately, although the Town Fire Brigade 'was early on the scene', their 'hose poured too weak a stream of water on the sheet of the flame'. It was only after the arrival of the Highland Railway Brigade and the Cameron Highlanders with more powerful hoses that the fire was finally brought under control.

The fire utterly destroyed the market, with the cost of the damage estimated at £12,000 (approximately £1.2 million today), not including the value of the stock that was lost. Thankfully, there was no loss of life other than that of a touchingly faithful dog belonging to Messrs A. & D. Macdonald, a butcher's shop in the market. The brave hound 'had been left in charge of [their] premises, and although an effort was made to get him to leave, he refused to quit, and was consequently burned to death at his post'.

Happily, it took a mere two years to rebuild the market. The new structure was opened to the public on 8 September, 1891 to much celebration. The market has gone from strength to strength in the years since, and is rightly a much-loved corner of Inverness.

Address Academy Street, Inverness, IV1 1JN, +44 (0)1463 710524, www.thevictorianmarket.co.uk | Getting there Bus 17, 27, 28, 28A, 307 and various others to Inverness Bus Station; train to Inverness; paid parking at Old Town Rose Street Car Park | Hours Market open Sun–Tue 8am–6pm, Wed–Sat 8am–8pm, individual business opening hours vary | Tip Ness Islands are a group of small natural islands in the River Ness just 30 minutes' walk from the Victorian Market. The two largest islands are linked to the mainland by Victorian footbridges.

# 42 Wardlaw Mausoleum
*Heading for trouble*

Wardlaw Mausoleum has been the resting place of the Lovat Fraser family since 1634. Its most famous inhabitant is Simon Fraser, 11th Lord Lovat, known by friends and enemies alike as the 'Old Fox'.

Fraser was born in 1667, the second son of Thomas Fraser of Beaufort and Lady Sybilla MacLeod. His rise to the top began by chance when his elder brother, Alexander, was killed at the Battle of Killiecrankie in 1689. He acquired the title of 11th Lord Lovat through a forced marriage with Amelia, Lady Lovat, widow of the 10th Lord Lovat. This so angered Lady Amelia's family that Fraser was forced to flee Scotland for France. It was there that he converted to Catholicism and fell in with the exiled Jacobites. However, for the next 40 or so years, Fraser cannily refused to commit fully to their cause, and even sided with the British government whenever that was advantageous.

Fraser havered during the Jacobite rising of 1745 too. It was only after the Jacobite victory at Prestonpans that he openly (and a touch cynically) declared his loyalty to the cause. This was unfortunate. After Culloden, Fraser found himself on the losing side. On 7 June, 1746 he was captured and taken to the Tower of London to stand trial for treason. Found guilty, he was sentenced to execution by being hanged, drawn and quartered. This was a particularly brutal way to die, with many victims still being alive and conscious as they were disembowelled. Fraser was spared this ordeal by King George II, who ordered death by beheading instead. His last words before the axe fell were *'Dulce et decorum est pro patria mori'* (It is sweet and proper to die for one's country).

Curiously, Fraser may not reside at Wardlaw. Recent analysis has shown that the body in Fraser's lead-lined coffin is that of an unknown woman. Where the remains of the 'Old Fox' actually lie is, for now, a delicious mystery.

Address Wardlaw Road, Kirkhill, Inverness, IV5 7NB, +44 (0)1463 831742, www.wardlawmausoleum.com | Getting there Take the Wardlaw Road turn-off from St Mary's Road/B 9164 and park in the small lay-by nearby | Hours Tours of the mausoleum by arrangement (see website for details) | Tip Visit nearby Beaufort Castle, built on land that was originally part of the Lovat Estate.

# 43 Applecross Pass
*White knuckle ride?*

There are a lot of scenic routes in Scotland, but arguably *the* most scenic is the Applecross Pass. It's also a *terrifying* route too, if you're a particularly nervous driver or have just passed your test – learning to drive on the pass is *not* recommended.

The Applecross Pass is the third highest road in Scotland, and has the greatest ascent of any road in Britain. Both ends of the pass start at sea level and it's a giddy 2,054-foot climb to the summit, the road winding its way to the top in a series of sweeping curves and hairpin bends. In places the gradient is twenty per cent, or one in five in old money. Just to make things more 'fun', the pass is largely single-track too, so drivers must be prepared to pull into a passing place whenever necessary (something that happens *frequently* in summer, as the road is on the NC500 route). Don't think you can use the pass all year round, however: it's often closed in winter when ice and snow make the going too dangerous.

The Gaelic name for the Applecross Pass is *Bealach na Bà*, which translates as the 'pass of the cattle'. The route has been used for centuries by cattle drovers to take their stock to market in Easter Ross, and further afield to Falkirk and even London. However, it's thought that people have been using the pass for nearly 2,000 years, most notably St Maelrubha and his disciples in the 7th century. The modern road has its origins in the efforts of the Mackenzie family in the early 19th century. The family owned huge swathes of land in the locale, and were keen to make their property more economically viable. Through links to government, the Mackenzies secured a substantial grant to build a road. Work began on 4 May, 1818, though, as legend has it, the first contractor slowly went insane from the difficulty of construction, and the attempt was soon abandoned. The road was eventually completed in 1822 by John Reid and Son, for a (then) very reasonable fee of £4000.

Address Start at either Applecross, IV54 8LR or Tornapress, IV54 8XE, hires.prefix.pillow and jars.redeeming.recall, respectively | Getting there Free car park at Applecross, with various viewpoints along the length of the route | Tip Applecross Photographic Gallery is owned by local photographer Jack Marris, and features his landscape photography shot in the local area.

# 44 Arctic Convoy Area
*Keeping a watch*

One of the more significant political events of the 1930s was the Treaty of Non-Aggression between Germany and the Union of Soviet Socialist Republics in 1939, less formally known as the Nazi-Soviet Pact. The treaty committed the two powers to economic co-operation, and included a pledge that neither country would attack the other for a period of at least 10 years. Nazi Germany and the Soviet Union were bitter enemies, so the agreement came as a shock to the governments of France and the United Kingdom.

The agreement lasted a mere two years. On 22 June, 1941, Hitler launched his invasion of the Soviet Union, codenamed Operation Barbarossa. On the principle that my enemy's enemy is my friend, the British Government pledged to support Russia in her fight to repel the Nazi invaders.

One form this support took was the supply of arms to the Soviets. These were transported by sea to the Russian ports of Archangel and Murmansk by Britain's Merchant Navy, escorted by Royal Navy warships. Unfortunately, to reach these ports the convoys of ships had to sail close to the northern coast of German-occupied Norway. The risk was enormous. The Arctic Convoys, as they were known, were under constant threat from German aircraft, U-boats and destroyers, as well as rough weather and sea ice. Losses were huge. By the end of the war, 3,500 allied servicemen had lost their lives, and 104 merchant ships and 24 warships had been sunk.

Loch Ewe is a deep sea loch that faces out into the North Atlantic. For four years the loch was the main base for the ships of the Arctic Convoys, with the coastline around the loch turned into a heavily guarded military area. At Rubha nan Sasan you can see the defensive buildings erected during the war: two gun batteries, searchlight emplacements and lookout posts. There is also a touching memorial stone commemorating those lost at sea in the Arctic Convoys.

THE RUSSIAN CONVOY CLUB

"IN MEMORY OF OUR SHIPMATES
WHO SAILED FROM LOCH EWE
DURING WORLD WAR II
THEY LOST THEIR LIVES
BITTER ARCTIC BATTLES
TO NORT
ND NEVER
S TRANQ

LOCHBROOM, ULLAPOOL
BRANCH

Arctic Convoy
OR

Address Achnasheen, IV22 2LT, nitrogen.divisible.earful | Getting there Take the
Inverasdale and Cove turn-off on the A 832 and follow the B 8057 to the Arctic Convoy
Area where you'll find free on-site parking | Tip Learn more about the fate of the men
and their ships at the Russian Arctic Convoy Museum.

# 45 Corrieshalloch Gorge

*Don't look down*

What's in a name? Corrieshalloch is Gaelic for 'ugly hollow'. Corrieshalloch Gorge is anything but. It is a mile-long box canyon gouged out of the bedrock by glacial meltwater towards the end of the last Ice Age, over 10,000 years ago. The rock is a mix of sedimentary mudstones and sandstones known as the Moine rocks. These rocks fracture easily and would have been no match for the raging torrents of water released when the glacier retreated. The River Droma, which runs through Corrieshalloch, is a pale ghost in comparison, but is still impressive after heavy rain.

Corrieshalloch Gorge was presented to the National Trust for Scotland in 1945 by John Calder of Ardargie. (Calder's generosity didn't end there, as he also gifted £1000 of brewery shares to the Trust in 1952.) Corrieshalloch was an immediate hit when it opened to the public. In 1952, the executive committee of the NTS discovered just how popular and appreciated the gorge actually was. At a committee meeting that year it was announced that a collection box erected at the site had received £20 in donations within a month of installation, the equivalent of £480 today.

Calder acquired Corrieshalloch (and the Braemore Estate) in the early 1920s from the Fowler family. The Victorian suspension bridge over the gorge was constructed by Sir John Fowler, who co-designed the (far larger!) Forth Bridge in Edinburgh. If you have a head for heights then you'll enjoy the view across to the Falls of Measach, which plunges 150 feet down in the dark depths of the gorge. If you don't have a head for heights then close your eyes and ask someone to guide you across.

Corrieshalloch Gorge has a damp microclimate that has helped a variety of ferns and mosses to thrive there. It has also helped the gorge attain the status of a Scottish national nature reserve, as well as being a Site of Special Scientific Interest.

**Address** Off the A 832 / A 835, Ullapool, IV23 2PJ, www.nts.org.uk, distanced.cascade.remaining | Getting there Paid car parks just off the A 832 and then a short (but steep) walk down into the gorge | Hours Corrieshalloch Gorge open daily; NTS Nature Centre and Café open daily 3 Jan – 28 Mar Wed – Sun 9.30am – 3pm, 29 Mar – 1 Nov 9.30am – 4pm | Tip The eastern Loch Droma viewpoint offers fine views of the loch and Beinn Liath Bheag.

# 46 — Cromarty Courthouse

*Porridge may be on the menu*

The Scottish Highlands and Islands are generally a safe place to live or to visit. The crime rate is low and has actually been slowly declining over the decades. The now-repurposed Georgian courthouse in the village of Cromarty is an interesting relic of a time when crime was a *far* more pressing concern in the region.

Cromarty Courthouse was commissioned by George Ross from Pitkerrie, Ross-shire. After time spent in Edinburgh as a lawyer, Ross moved to London, where he made his fortune as an army agent, a civilian who recruited men for Britain's military. It was this wealth that allowed him to purchase the title deeds of the Cromarty estate in 1767, and then to embark on the task of improving the town. According to Hugh Miller in *Scenes and Legends of the North of Scotland* (1850), Ross was 'fully determined' that 'if he but lived long enough, to make Cromarty worth an Englishman's while coming all the way from London to see'.

In Miller's view, Ross had 'presented the town with a neat substantial building'. Miller also wrote that the upper part 'still serves for a council-room and court-house, and the lower as a prison'. Work on the exterior was complete by 1773, though curiously it took another 10 years before the interior was fully outfitted.

Three new cells and an area for daily exercise were added to the courthouse between 1845 and 1847. Ironically, however, the population of Cromarty declined in the following decades. The courthouse ceased to be a county prison in 1879, and the cells were last used during World War I by the Naval Shore Patrol, when Cromarty was home to a naval base. The courthouse is now a truly fascinating museum, one that vividly brings to life the history of the building. You can thrill to a recreation of a trial in the courtroom, visit a prisoner in his cell, and listen to eccentric genius Sir Thomas Urquhart. It's a place you will want to do… *spend* time in.

Address Church Street, Cromarty, IV11 8XA, +44 (0)1381 600418, www.cromarty-courthouse.org.uk | Getting there Bus 21, 21A, 26, 26A, 126 or 424 to Victoria Hall; take the A 832 to Cromarty, park on Shore Street and then a short walk | Hours Daily Apr–Oct noon–4pm | Tip Fort George is an extensive 18th-century garrison built after the Jacobite rising of 1745. It's still a working army barracks, though areas of the fort are open to visitors.

# 47 __ Cromarty Firth
*The fourth firth north of the Firth of Forth*

A firth is a stretch of sea projecting inland to create a salt water inlet, similar to – but not quite the same as – an estuary. The term derives from the Old Norse word *fjǫrðr*, from which the modern Norwegian word fjord originated. (The word estuary has its origins in the Latin *aestuarium*, in case you were wondering.) Firth is more commonly used on the east coast of Scotland than the west, and more rarely still in England. Sea lochs in the northern Highlands are essentially firths, though curiously they are never referred to as such.

The Black Isle forms the southern edge of the Cromarty Firth. Confusingly, the Black Isle is not an island, but a peninsula. Why it has the name it does is something of a mystery. One explanation is that it's a corruption of the Gaelic *eilean dubh*, which translates as black isle. This does not of course solve the puzzle, but pushes it further back in history. The 'black' part of the name may refer to the rich, dark soil of the Black Isle. But it may not. Another theory has it that the mountains to the north are usually snow covered in winter, whereas the Black Isle generally remains snow free.

The Cromarty Firth has a strangely dual character. Cromarty itself, at the mouth of the firth on its southern shore, is a charming and friendly village. Directly opposite on the northern shore is the Port of Nigg. This is a huge deepwater facility, built to serve the needs of the energy industry. The most important of these industries is North Sea oil and gas. The evidence for this are the oil rigs parked in the firth. These giant steel structures are usually there for repair work or servicing at either the Port of Nigg or at Invergordon further east. Some are also waiting to be decommissioned. The future for North Sea oil is increasingly uncertain; offshore wind farms are increasingly important to the Scottish economy. Cannily, the Port of Nigg also offers storage space for wind turbine towers and blades before they're shipped out to sea for installation.

Address Cromarty, IV11 8YL | Getting there Bus 21, 21A, 26, 26A, 126 or 424 to Victoria Hall; take the A 832 to Cromarty and park on Shore Street | Tip The Nigg stone inside Nigg Old Church is a wonderfully intricate carved Pictish stone that was created in the 8th century.

# 48 Eilean Donan
*Family seat*

At the confluence of three lochs – the Long, Duich and Alsh – is a small island on top of which sits the castle of Eilean Donan. If any castle can be said to be *the* quintessential Highland castle it is Eilean Donan. It has featured in many TV shows and movies, including the James Bond movie *The World is Not Enough*, as well as on the packaging of countless products such as whisky and shortbread.

The first castle on the site was built in the 13th century by Alexander II as a defence against Viking raids. The castle later came into the possession of the Mackenzies of Kintail, who garrisoned men of MacRae and MacLennan clans there. After 500 eventful years, the original castle was ruined in 1719 after bombardment by government frigates in the aftermath of the first Jacobite rising. It was rescued in the early 20th century by Lieutenant Colonel John MacRae-Gilstrap, head of the MacRae family of Conchra.

A short letter written by John after he bought Eilean Donan is reproduced in *Ella's War: From a MacRae Archive* by family member Fiona Christina MacRae. Dated 19 February, 1913, the note reads, 'Just a few lines to let you know that I have now acquired the island and the Castle of Eilean Donan in Kintail sound, which has centred on clan history for five centuries'.

Working closely with architect George Mackie Watson and local clerk of works Farquhar MacRae, John spent the following two decades lovingly restoring Eilean Donan. It's said that the plan for the restoration came to Farquhar in a dream in which he saw the rebuilt castle in all its glory. Work was completed in 1932 with the building of an arched bridge to connect the island to the mainland. John died in 1936 at the age of 76 and was buried in the MacRae cemetery at Clachan Duich. The castle opened to the public in 1955. It is now in the care of the Conchra Charitable Trust, created by the MacRae family in 1983.

Address Dornie, by Kyle of Lochalsh, IV40 8DX, +44 (0)1599 555202, www.eileandonancastle.com | Getting there Bus 915, 916 or 917 to Bridge Road End; paid parking at the castle just off the A 87 | Hours Check website for hours | Tip Plockton is known as the 'Jewel of the Highlands' and was memorably used as a location in the horror movie classic *The Wicker Man*.

# 49 __ Fainmore House
*Tuber troubles*

On an empty moor at the western end of the A 832 is a lonesome building, obviously long deserted. This is Fainmore House and there is a curious mystery as to its original purpose. One theory is that it once served as an inn, keeping passing cattle drovers fed and watered. An Ordnance Survey map of the area (Sheet 92 – Inverbroom), surveyed in 1874 and published in 1881, has a Fain Inn marked in the same place as Fainmore House.

What's odd is that Fainmore House doesn't look much like an inn, even allowing for its current derelict state (the jaunty orange-red corrugated roof is a later addition). The National Record of the Historic Environment states that Fainmore is (or rather was) a shepherd's house. Whichever it is, there's a nobility to the building, stuck out in the middle of nowhere all on its own.

The A 832 is something of a record holder. It's 125 miles in length and connects Cromarty on the east coast to Gairloch on the west, and Gairloch to Corrieshalloch Gorge and a junction with the A 835. It's the longest road in Britain that sticks entirely within the boundaries of a single county (Ross and Cromarty), and is the longest triple-digit A-road in Scotland. It's also a wonderfully scenic route that shouldn't be rushed, but savoured.

The Fainmore stretch of the A 832 was originally known as the 'Destitution Road'. It was built in the late 1840s by poor and desperate Highlanders. Potatoes had long been the staple diet of many a family. In 1843 and 1845, a blight seriously affected potato crops. A third wave of potato blight in 1848 led to the very real threat of starvation across the Highlands. The 'Destitution Road' was devised as a way to hand out rations of oats to the men, women and children who were prepared to work on its construction. It was a hard life, but one that prevented death on a similar scale to that seen in Ireland during that country's contemporaneous potato famine.

Address Off the A832, IV23 2RY, heartened.patrolled.destroyer | Getting there Limited off-road parking nearby | Hours Accessible 24 hours | Tip Look to the north-west and (weather permitting) you'll see the mountain group of An Teallach, the two highest peaks of which – Bidean a' Ghlas Thuill and Sgùrr Fiona – qualify as Munros.

# 50__Fyrish Monument
*Keynesian economics?*

John Maynard Keynes is arguably the most influential economist of the 20th century. In 1936, he published his *General Theory of Employment, Interest and Money*. The Great Depression of the 1930s, precipitated by the stock market crash of 1929, had caused high unemployment across Britain. Until Keynes, it was thought that unemployment rates would only fall if workers were prepared to accept lower wages. Keynes believed that factories would not employ workers if the goods they produced could not be sold. He persuasively argued that the government should intervene financially to kick-start the economy. Employers would then employ more workers as demand for goods and services increased. This was radical stuff for the time. However, it wasn't an entirely new idea…

The Fyrish Monument is a huge stone folly, built in 1782 at the summit of Fyrish Hill. It was commissioned by Sir Hector Munro, 8th Laird of Navor. Munro was a career soldier in the British Army, who made his name mopping up Jacobite resistance in the Highlands in the decade after Culloden. In 1761, he arrived in India as head of the 89th (Highland Regiment of Foot). He led his troops to victory at the Battle of Buxar in 1764 against a far larger Mughal army. In 1768, Munro returned to Scotland a hero and was elected as MP for the Inverness Burghs.

The design of the Fyrish Monument is based on the Gates of Negapatam (now Nagapattinam), which Munro besieged in October 1781 during a second stint in India. Munro had the folly built to employ labourers affected by the clearances, with the workers paid a penny a day for their services. A local legend has it that Munro would occasionally have the stone rolled back down the hill. This delayed completion of the monument and so kept the workers in employment for longer, a far-sighted and noble strategy that Keynes would surely have approved of.

Address Alness, IV16 9XL, torso.helpless.pumpkin | Getting there Free parking off the Boath Road (appraised.followers.breaches) just off the B 1976 and then a (steep) one-hour walk to the monument | Hours Accessible 24 hours | Tip Black Rock Gorge near Evanton is a deep box canyon that was used as a filming location for *Harry Potter and the Goblet of Fire*.

# 51   Highland Cows
*Beefy beasties*

What's the first thing that pops into your head when you think of the Highlands? Give it a go right now! Was it a Highland cow by any chance? You wouldn't be alone if it were. Highland cows are a much-loved and iconic creature, as much a part of the Scottish landscape as the mountains and camper vans.

The Highland cow, or 'heilan coo', is one of the oldest cattle breeds in the world. Originally, there were two classes: the West Highlander (or Kyloe) and the Highlander. Kyloes originated on the western isles, and were smaller than modern cattle. They were also predominantly either black or brindled (an animal with a dark brown coat that has dark flecks or streaks). The two classes are now no longer recognised. Today, the breed is simply Highland.

There are Gaelic terms to describe the colours of Highland cattle. A yellow male is *buidhe*, a yellow female is *bhuidhe*. *Donn* describes a brown (or dun) laddie, and *dhonn* a brown lassie. A less colourful Highland is *dubh* (male) or *dhubh* (female) when black, or *geal* (male) or *gheal* (female) when white. The Highland Cattle Society encourages its members to use the Gaelic descriptions when naming individuals in a herd (or more correctly, a fold), so Alastair Donn would be a brown male, and Ailsa Bhuidhe his yellow female friend. Whatever the colour, it's the coat of the Highland that's the secret to the breed's success. A Highland's coat has two layers. The upper layer – the overcoat, if you like – is thick and long and oily, which helps rain and snow slip off. Underneath is a downy undercoat, which helps keep the beastie warm, whatever the weather.

What's surprising about Highland cattle is just how placid they are; those big, sharp horns belie their sweet nature. That doesn't mean that you should get up close and personal, though. No one is entirely sure whether Highlands can see through the long fringe that covers their eyes. So, accidents can happen…

**Address** Highland cattle are widespread across the Scottish Highland area. Look out for them around Duirinish and Plockton, Bealach na Bà between Applecross and Shieldaig, and on Clachtoll Beach where they often nibble on the seaweed | **Tip** One place you're guaranteed to see Highland cows is the Trossachs Woollen Mill in Kilmahog, which has its own resident herd.

# 52 Hugh Miller's Cottage
*Geology genius*

On 10 October, 1802, Harriet Wright, wife of Hugh Millar, gave birth to a son. The infant was named after his father, though his surname was later changed to Miller. The cottage in Cromarty in which Hugh was born has been preserved and, along with a splendid museum next door, is open to the public.

According to the 1862 biography *Life of Hugh Miller, a Sketch for Working Men* by Samuel Partridge, Miller 'was descended from a long line of seafaring men'. This included the elder Hugh, who was a shipmaster and who would die in 1807 in a shipwreck. Raised by the widowed Harriet and two maternal uncles, James and Alexander, Miller was educated in a parish school. It was there that he learnt to read, first from the *Bible*, and then from 'an abundance of profane classics' such as 'Jack the Giant Killer' and 'Beauty and the Beast'. At the age of 17, Miller was apprenticed to a stonemason. It was while working with stone from local quarries that 'his attention was fairly aroused and his interest awakened with reference to geology'. It was this new passion that was to make his name.

In 1841, Miller wrote *The Old Red Sandstone*, a description of the sedimentary rock found on the eastern coast of Scotland. The rock was laid down during the Devonian period, roughly 416 to 359 million years ago. It is a time known as the 'Age of Fishes' due to the diversity of fish species that evolved then. One Devonian species, *Pterichthyodes milleri*, was discovered by and named after Miller.

Although conservative and deeply religious, Miller believed in an ancient Earth. He thought that the 'days' of creation referred to in the 'Book of Genesis' represented geological periods rather than a literal 24 hours. However, Miller rejected the concept of evolution proposed by Jean-Baptiste Lamarck in the early 1800s. For him, fossils demonstrated the exquisite design skills of a benevolent God, preserved for eternity in stone.

Address Hugh Miller's Birthplace Cottage and Museum, Church Street, Cromarty, Ross-shire, IV11 8XA, +44 (0)1381 600245, www.nts.org.uk | Getting there Take the A832 to Cromarty, park on Shore Street and then a short walk | Hours Apr–Oct Wed–Sun 11am–4pm (see website for details) | Tip Walk the Hugh Miller Trail, starting near Eathie Mains, to see where Miller found his first fossils.

# 53 Inverewe Gardens
*Impossible is just a word*

On 18 June, 1863, the *Inverness Courier* noted that 'the estate of Inverewe, in the parish of Gairloch, Ross-shire, lately the property of Sir William Mackenzie, Bt, of Coul, has been sold to Osgood Hanbury Mackenzie, Esq., son of the late Sir Francis Mackenzie of Gairloch'. Osgood, and later his daughter, Mairi Sawyer, would transform the estate, creating an 'impossible' garden on an unpromising rocky peninsula that still thrives to this day.

Osgood faced many challenges when planning his garden. Salt-tinged winds are a feature of the area, and the thinness of the estate's soil was also far from ideal. Osgood elegantly solved the first of his problems by planting a mix of trees and shrubs, such as Douglas Fir and Corsican pine, to create a windbreak for the garden. The second difficulty was sorted by importing soil from elsewhere, and digging in seaweed to add nutrients.

Osgood devoted the rest of his life to his garden, planting a wide variety of exotic flora from around the world. He had one factor in his favour. Despite Inverewe's northerly latitude, the climate is relatively equable all year round due to the warming influence of the Gulf Stream. Osgood died on 15 April, 1922, with his only child Mairi inheriting his estate.

Mairi improved the garden further; the Rock Garden, Coronation Knoll and ponds are her work. She also opened the garden to visitors. A notice in *The Aberdeen Press and Journal* on 17 August, 1933 informed readers that Inverewe Gardens were 'full of the most interesting rare shrubs, will be opened to the public on Saturday, August 19, from 2 p.m. to 6 p.m. A charge of 1s will be made for admission, and 1s for cars.' The proceeds of this event went to the Maintenance Fund of the Royal Northern Infirmary. Mairi gifted the gardens to the National Trust for Scotland in 1952. The Trust has diligently and sensitively looked after them ever since.

Address Poolewe, Achnasheen, IV22 2LG, +44 (0)1445 712950, www.nts.org.uk | Getting there Bus 700, 700A or 707 to Inverewe Gardens; just off the A 832 with parking on-site (fee payable) | Hours Gardens daily 1–28 Mar 10am–4pm, 29 Mar–15 Nov 10am–5pm; Visitor Centre daily 29 Mar–15 Nov 9.30am–4.30pm | Tip Look north from the Inverewe Viewpoint on the A 832 to see the most romantically named island in Scotland: Isle of Ewe.

# 54 Invergordon Murals
*Painting the town red (and blue and green)*

It was the turn of the Millennium, and Marion Rhind had a great idea. She had recently heard from her parents about Sheffield, a rural town in Tasmania. In the 1980s, Sheffield's local council decided to improve the town's fortunes by painting murals on the sides of buildings. The plan worked and the murals brought in hundreds of thousands of visitors each year, turning Sheffield into a thriving tourist destination. Rhind had the notion that a similar scheme would work its magic on her home town of Invergordon, which was suffering from high unemployment. A member of the Invergordon business association, Rhind believed that 'we needed some kind of draw to bring people off the liners into the town'.

Fast forward five years and much behind-the-scenes work… In 2007, the Off the Wall committee had the funds to start the project in earnest. Invergordon's various community groups were invited to suggest themes and subjects for the murals. Artists were brought in from across the world to meet the locals, and to get to know the town. Proposals for murals were created and voted on. After much deliberation five artists and their designs were chosen. And so scaffolding was erected and the painting got underway.

On 4 September, 2007, Princess Anne officially launched the Invergordon Mural Trail. On the day of the launch, the Princess Royal was greeted at each mural by a member of the Off the Wall committee, as well as representatives of the community group associated with the mural. There are 11 murals on the trail, each illustrating a particular aspect of life in Invergordon. Perhaps the most moving is *The Long Goodbye* by Tracey Shough. The multi-panel work shows the Seaforth Highlanders, 51st Highland Division, leaving for war in France in 1939 and the events that led to their defeat and eventual surrender at St Valery-en-Caux in 1940.

Sadly, Marion died in July 2021, but her legacy lives on.

116

Address The murals can be found on buildings all around Invergordon, www.invergordonoffthewall.org.uk | Getting there Bus 7, 23A, 25, 25A or X25 to Cameron's Garden Centre; train to Invergordon; take the B 817 – free car park on Bank Street | Hours Accessible 24 hours | Tip Learn more about life in Invergordon and the Cromarty Firth area at the Invergordon Naval Museum and Heritage Centre.

# 55 Loch Torridon
*Let's buy an estate*

An advert in the *Inverness Courier* dated 1 October, 1818 drew the reader's attention to a 'Capital and Valuable Freehold Estate, Ross-Shire', which was to be sold in lot by a Mr Hoggart at the end of that month in London. The 'Torridon Estate, within the parish of Applecross' amounted to 'Twenty Thousand Acres of Land' and included a salmon and herring fishery, and was 'abundantly stocked with Ptarmigan, Grouse, Red Deer, and Roe'. The buyer would gain himself (and it would have been a him) 'in every respect a valuable domain for Sporting'.

Hunting, shooting and fishing is still an important part of Highland life. A party out for a day's sport is usually guided by a gillie (or ghillie), an old Gaelic term for a servant or attendant. Gillies originally served Highland chiefs, doing all the dirty work for the chief including such duties as carrying him over burns or boggy moorland (why should the boss get his feet wet?). A gillie is someone with a deep and intimate knowledge of the landscape, who knows where herds of deer gather or where the best salmon fishing on a river is to be had. The best-known gillie in history is John Brown, who was a favourite of Queen Victoria and who faithfully served the monarch for 34 years. The inscription on a memorial to Brown at Balmoral reads *Friend more than Servant. Loyal. Truthful. Brave. Self less than Duty, even to the Gra*ve.

Loch Torridon is a sea loch and is home to a variety of fish, including mackerel and pollack. However, you can't just wander down to the shoreline with your rod and start fishing. The right to fish belongs to the landowner, and his (or her in these more enlightened times) permission must be obtained first. Another fish found in Loch Torridon is salmon. These magnificent creatures are spawned in the rivers that flow into the loch, making their way out into the North Atlantic when mature.

Address Torridon, Achnasheen, IV22 2EZ, www.visittorridon.co.uk | Getting there Bus 705 to Hall or Youth Hostel (Torridon) or 702, 704 or 705 to Telephone Kiosk (Shieldaig); just off the A 896 for limited on-street parking in the villages around Loch Torridon | Tip The Gille Brighde Restaurant in Lower Diabaig prides itself on using fresh, locally sourced and seasonal ingredients. Booking a table beforehand is recommended as the road back to the nearest town is long and winding, particularly if you're hungry.

# 56 MacFarquhar's Bed
*No rest for the wicked*

Scotland has its fair share of odd and unusual place names. Perthshire boasts Dull, a village playfully twinned with Boring in Oregon (both are members of the League of Extraordinary Communities, along with Bland in Australia). You can find Lost in Aberdeenshire (or can you?). There's a Glutton, a Boor, an Inchlumpie and a Bad Bog in Ross and Cromarty. Teapot in the Trossachs sounds more tempting than Old Scone, though Jam might help. And in North Lanarkshire there's the delightfully bonkers Bonkle.

In such company, MacFarquhar's Bed sounds vaguely sensible as place names go. However, there is no bed there, or at least not the kind you could sleep in. And no one now knows who MacFarquhar was. One possibility is that he was a smuggler who operated in the area, though what he smuggled is now lost to history. We don't even know whether he was successful at his chosen profession or whether the authorities ever caught him in the act.

MacFarquhar's Bed is a geological feature: an outcrop of the Raddery Sandstone Formation, laid down some 380 million years ago. What remains now after aeons of erosion is a jagged triangular slab of rock that erupts from the ground like a shark's tooth, a slender and entirely natural stone arch, and a shallow sea cave. Look closely at the stone and you'll see that it has a definite pebbly texture, which is an easily identifiable characteristic of Raddery sandstone.

Hugh Miller was a visitor to MacFarquhar's Bed. In *The Life and Letters of Hugh Miller* (1871) Miller recorded that 'Before leaving MacFarquhar's Bed, I had a delightful bathe among the rocks'. Unfortunately, he obviously misjudged the strength of the waves for he then lamented that 'On landing I was dashed against a rock, and had to walk very softly for three days after, lest I should be asked whether I was not lame'. Whether he had a Moan about the experience afterwards was sadly unrecorded.

Address Cromarty, Strathpeffer, IV14 9EW, later.beats.untruth | Getting there Limited off-road parking near Cromarty Mains Farm (satin.displays.offline) and then a 30-minute walk | Tip Take a keek at the mouth of the Cromarty Firth from the South Sutor View Point.

# 57 _ Peach and Horne
*Unravelling the mysteries of Earth*

At its most basic, stratigraphy is the scientific study of rock layers (or 'strata'). In a perfect world, the oldest layers of rock would always be found at the bottom of a cliff or hill and the youngest layers at the top. Unfortunately, we don't live in a perfect world and sometimes the chronological order is reversed or even jumbled.

This untidiness puzzled geologists in the 19th century. In his three-volume work of 1819, *A Description of the Western Isles of Scotland*, John MacCulloch asked a very reasonable question: 'How is it possible for gneiss, the oldest rock in the British Isles, a rock that has spent thousands of years below the Earth's crust being squeezed and heated, to end up lying on top of rocks that are almost unchanged from the day they were laid down on the Earth's surface?'

Geologist Roderick Murchison had an answer. Murchison made his reputation in Wales in 1831, after identifying a new geological period he named the Silurian. Intrigued by reports of fossils found in Durness, Murchison travelled to the Highlands in 1855, accompanied by fellow geologist James Nicol. On seeing similar oddly transposed rock strata as MacCulloch, Murchison came to the conclusion that there was no problem: the layers of gneiss were younger than the strata below and therefore in the right chronological order. Nicol disagreed with this assessment. He believed that a geological fault had lifted the older layers above the younger. Murchison was the more esteemed of the two and so his argument prevailed.

This was known as the 'Highland Controversy'. It was only resolved by Doctors Ben Peach and John Horne, who extensively surveyed Assynt on behalf of the British Geological Survey in 1882. The two men soon discovered that Nicol was essentially right: older rock (formed elsewhere) had been thrust over younger rock, confusing the layer order. A lively statue of the pair at Knockan Crag celebrates their magnificent scientific achievement.

Address Knockan Crag, Elphin, IV27 4HH, +44 (0)1463 701600, www.nature.scot, smuggled.quaking.kneeled | Getting there Bus 809 to Knockan Crag; free parking at the Knockan Crag National Nature Reserve Car Park just off the A 835 | Tip The Knockan Crag National Nature Reserve is home to a wide variety of birds such as eagles, buzzards, ravens and kestrels, as well as lizards and frogs.

# 58 Ullapool Clock
## *Tick tock star*

Everyone who has a mobile phone also has a camera. People whose job it is to know these things reckon that some 1.81 trillion photos are now shot worldwide every year. That's 57,000 per second! And those numbers are expected to increase year-on-year over the coming decade. A good proportion of these photos (and videos) are posted on social media platforms such as Facebook and Instagram. This has led to certain beautiful or iconic locations becoming *the* place to take a photo or two.

Ullapool's splendidly ornate and handsome village clock is just such a place. It is said – understandably – to be the most photographed clock in the Scottish Highlands. The clock is more formally known as the Fowler Memorial Clock. The first Fowler with a connection to Ullapool was Sir John Fowler, 1st Baronet of Braemore. Sir John was a *very* busy Victorian engineer, who specialised in large railway projects. He worked on London's Metropolitan Railway, the world's first underground railway line, as well as on regional lines such as the Stockton and Hartlepool Railway. Arguably, Sir John's greatest achievement was the Forth Railway Bridge, completed in 1890. Now on the UNESCO World Heritage List, this magnificent structure continues to carry trains safely and efficiently over the Firth of Forth.

The clock was gifted to the town in 1922 by Lady Alice Fowler, Sir John's daughter-in-law. It commemorates Sir John, as well as Alice's husband, Sir John Arthur Fowler, 2nd Baronet of Braemore, and her son, Captain Alan Fowler who died in 1915 during World War I. Lady Alice thoughtfully invested £100 to pay for maintenance on the clock. The clock was originally hand-wound by a volunteer from the village. The last person with that honour was local butcher Sandy Ross. In 1995, the clock mechanism was electrified and since then has kept excellent time.

Address 1 Argyle Street, Ullapool, IV26 2UB | Getting there Bus 809 or 811 to Latheron Lane Car Park; take the A 835 to Ullapool and park at the Latheron Lane Car Park | Tip The Ullapool Museum has an extensive collection of objects and records that show how the people of the Lochbroom region have lived over the centuries.

# 59 Alexander McQueen Grave
*Style guru*

Lewisham in London is a long way from Kilmuir on Skye in so many ways. The man who connects the two is Lee Alexander McQueen, who is regarded as one of the most influential fashion designers of modern times. McQueen was born in the London borough on 17 March, 1969 to Ron, a (Scottish) taxi driver, and Joyce, who taught social science. He showed a flair for design at an early age by creating dresses for his three older sisters.

At the age of 16, McQueen was apprenticed to Anderson & Sheppard, a men's tailors on Savile Row. It was there that he first learnt traditional tailoring techniques, creating bespoke suits for the likes of Mikhail Gorbachev and Prince Charles. McQueen followed this by working for notable designers Koji Tatsuno in Mayfair and Romeo Gigli in Milan. Returning to London, McQueen enrolled at Central Saint Martins College of Art & Design, where he was awarded an MA in fashion design in 1992.

It was McQueen's graduation collection, *Jack the Ripper Stalks his Victims*, that made his name in the fashion industry. Leading stylist Isabella Blow was so impressed by the show that she bought the entire collection, and later became a friend and mentor to McQueen. In the years that followed, McQueen launched his own eponymous clothing business (dropping his first name on the advice of Blow, though he was always Lee to family and friends), and worked as Chief Designer for French fashion house Givenchy for five years.

Two deaths weighed heavily on McQueen. In 2007, Blow committed suicide. This was followed by the death of his beloved mother on 2 February, 2010. Suffering from depression and anxiety, McQueen killed himself eight days later. By request, his ashes were buried in Kilmuir Cemetery, a statement by his family noting that 'Lee cherished the times that he was able to spend on the Isle of Skye – he enjoyed the beauty, peace and tranquillity'.

LEE
ALEXANDER
McQUEEN
1969 2010
C·B·E

Address Kilmuir Cemetery, Hunglader, IV51 9YU, denoting.tadpole.contacts | Getting there Take the Kilmuir Cemetery turn-off on the A855 and park outside the cemetery | Hours Accessible 24 hours | Tip Just a few minutes' drive north, the ruins of Duntulm Castle overlook the Little Minch (the sea that separates the Outer Hebrides from Skye).

# 60 Angus MacAskill
*Gentle giant*

In 1825, on a date now lost to posterity, a boy was born in Siabaidh on the Scottish island of Berneray. He was the son of Norman MacAskill and his wife Christina. Norman was five feet nine inches tall and described as 'stout', Christina meanwhile was said to be 'good-sized'. The couple named their new son Angus. He was the fourth of 12 children born to Norman and Christina, several of whom did not make it to adulthood. Angus was a small child and not expected to live. But somehow, wonderfully, he did.

Jump forward six years. The Highland clearances are in full swing and the MacAskill family are forced to leave their home. Like many other dispossessed Highlanders of the time, they headed for North America to make a new life for themselves. They settled in St Ann's on the island of Cape Breton in Nova Scotia. At this time, young Angus was still considered to be wee compared with his brothers. That changed when he hit his teenage years. It was then that he put on a growth spurt, which continued, and continued. By the time he was in his 20s, Angus was seven feet nine inches tall and weighed over 425 pounds. He was also incredibly strong, able to lift 350-pound barrels of flour with ease.

The term for excessive growth is gigantism, and it is often the result of a disorder that causes an overabundance of growth hormone during childhood. Robert Wadlow, the tallest person who has ever lived, suffered from a hypertrophy of the pituitary gland. This caused his height to reach eight feet eleven inches by the time he died at the age of 22. Angus did *not* suffer from a similar disorder, and was recognised in the 1981 edition of *The Guinness Book of Records* as the tallest non-pathological (or true) giant in history.

By far the best place to find out more about Angus is the Giant MacAskill Museum in Dunvegan. You can compare yourself with a life-sized model of Angus there, and see how you measure up.

**Address** 41 Kilmuir Road, Dunvegan, IV55 8WA, +44 (0)1470 521296, www.dunveganmuseums.co.uk | Getting there Bus to 56 or 56X to Museum; free parking at Dunvegan Car Park just off the A 863 | Hours Daily Easter–Oct 9.30am–6pm | Tip The Duirinish Stone near the ruined St Mary's Church may look ancient but was erected early this century by the community of Dunvegan.

# 61 Dinosaur Footprints

*Sandy claws*

It's a curious quirk of history that dinosaur is used as a synonym for something outdated or obsolete. Dinosaurs were around for some 165 million years before the line (with the exception of avian dinosaurs – birds) was wiped out by an asteroid at the end of the Cretaceous Period. In comparison, Hominins – that's us and our immediate ancestors – have been around for just seven million years. When the first dinosaur was discovered in 1819 it was thought to be a slow, lumbering sort of creature. Many different species of dinosaur were discovered after that, but the idea that they were a bit rubbish prevailed, particularly in comparison to mammals.

It wasn't until the late 1960s that this idea began to change. Today, dinosaurs are seen for what they truly were: an extraordinarily successful and varied set of creatures perfectly adapted to the world they lived in. If it hadn't been for that pesky asteroid striking Earth 65 million years ago, dinosaurs would in all probability still dominate the planet; mammals would have remained small nocturnal things, scratching out a living in the shadow of giants.

Most of what scientists know about dinosaurs is through their fossilised remains. These are typically the hard parts of an animal, such as the bones and teeth; the soft parts usually rot away or are scavenged. However, almost as important are trace fossils. These record the activities of an animal, and include fossilised faeces (known as coprolites), nests or burrows, and footprints.

A wonderfully preserved set of dinosaur footprints was found on An Corran beach in 2002. These remarkable tracks are some 170 million years old and were made by a species of Megalosaurus, a bipedal carnivore. There are 17 footprints in total and it's thought that the animal was just ambling along at a stately two miles an hour. After all, with the age of the dinosaurs barely begun, this particular Megalosaurus had all the time in the world.

Address An Corran Beach near Staffin, IV51 9JT, servants.dots.menswear | Getting there Free parking on An Corran Beach road | Hours Accessible 24 hours (tide and weather permitting) | Tip Learn more about prehistoric creatures and their fossils at the Staffin Dinosaur Museum.

# 62 Elgol

*Go for the history, stay for the view*

It's a long and winding drive to Elgol, but the route is wonderfully scenic and the destination is delightful. Elgol is a fishing village on Loch Scavaig at the northern end of the Strathaird Peninsula. The name is an Anglicised version of the Gaelic *Ealaghol*. This is thought to refer to Aella, an Anglo-Saxon warlord who supported Vortigern in the latter's 5th-century campaign for supremacy over the Picts and Scots. Five ships under the command of Aella fought a battle with the natives on Loch Scavaig. However, there is no concrete evidence for this other than it is a tale long told.

Elgol's less dubious claim to historical noteworthiness is found in the shape of Prince Charles' Cave, a short though very uneven walk south from the village. On 4 July, 1746, Charles Stuart spent his last night on Skye hiding in the cave. The following morning the prince, in the company of John MacKinnon and four boatmen, sailed back to the mainland. Avoiding capture for a further two months, Charles Stuart finally set sail for France and safety on 19 September, 1746. The cave is not the most salubrious accommodation on Skye and can only be safely reached during the two hours either side of low tide. Check the tide tables before setting off, otherwise you might have to spend a night in the cave too. You really *don't* want to be forced do that.

On the far side of Loch Scavaig is the Black Cuillin ridge. This is a series of 27 jagged mountains, 12 of which are Munros. Traversing the ridge is only for those with extensive mountaineering experience. It is a primal place, considered to be the hardest and most challenging mountain experience in Britain. Navigation is difficult too as the ferromagnetic rock affects compass readings, and GPS can be unreliable. Despite this, on 12 October, 2013, mountain runner Finlay Wild traversed the ridge in an astonishing 2 hours, 59 minutes and 22 seconds.

Address Elgol, IV49 9BG, hound.happen.fantastic | Getting there Bus 55 or 612 to Community Centre; off the B 8083 from Broadford – free parking at Elgol Car Park | Tip Take a boat trip from Elgol to Loch Coruisk (and back again) with Misty Isle Boat Trips. On the voyage you may well see basking sharks, dolphins, minke whales and seals.

# 63 Fairy Pools
*Crystal clear*

On 9 August, 2017, *The Guardian* published a thoughtful piece with the headline 'Skye islanders call for help with overcrowding after tourism surge'. The report noted that 'After decades of relative isolation and depopulation, Skye has recently become a must-see destination for hundreds of thousands of overseas visitors'. The increase in tourists was 'driven by Hollywood, pop stars, commercials and social media', and had led to traffic jams and an increase in litter.

One place overrun was the Fairy Pools, a series of waterfalls and deep pools on the Allt Coir' a' Mhadaidh, or the Burn of the Corrie of the Wolf. The two striking qualities of the pools are their clarity – the water is startlingly clear – and their blue-green tint. The pools can also be bitterly cold, even in summer. This seems not to discourage wild swimmers, who are often as blue as the water after their dip. They share the space with the fairies who are said to live in the glen, and who also like to bathe in the pools.

The Fairy Pools were the location of a clan battle in 1601. This was the bloody climax of a long-running feud between the Clan MacLeod of Dunvegan and the Clan MacDonald of Sleat. The MacLeod Laird had previously offered his sister's hand in marriage to the MacDonald Laird. The couple lived together for a year on the expectation that the wedding would only proceed if a son was born during that time. No child was forthcoming and the young woman had also become blind in one eye. She was sent back in disgrace, which infuriated the MacLeods. The only option was war. The subsequent Battle of Coire Na Creiche was won by the MacDonalds and proved to be the last clan battle on Skye.

As for tourism, Skye is still a busy place. However, thanks to careful investment, *some* of the problems are being solved. A new car park (with a one-way system) and footpath have thankfully made a visit to the Fairy Pools less fraught than it was in 2017.

Address Glenbrittle, IV47 8TA, podcast.including.retail | Getting there Paid parking at the Forestry Commission Car Park and then a 40-minute walk | Tip Fairy Glen is another mystically named place on Skye. The curiously conical mounds in the glen do look as though they were created by magical means. They were, however, created by an ancient landslip, similar to that which shaped the Trotternish Ridge.

# 64 Flora MacDonald Monument

*'Speed, bonnie boat, like a bird on the wing'*

After the bloody disaster of Culloden, it's understandable that Charles Stuart felt the need to flee. He sailed to the Outer Hebrides after making his way to the west coast of Scotland, ironically missing two French ships that had come to rescue him. Once safely over the Minch, Charles evaded capture by moving from island to island. He had a number of adventures during this time, including a period of near starvation and almost drowning at sea.

However, it was a meeting on South Uist that led to what may be the strangest event of the entire affair. On 28 June, 1746, Charles was introduced to Flora MacDonald. For reasons now lost, Flora agreed to assist Charles and get him safely to Skye. This was easier said than done, however, as a passport was now needed. Somehow Flora managed to obtain one from her stepfather. Charles then affected a disguise for the voyage. Under the name of Betty Burke and dressed as a maid, Charles boarded a rowing boat with Flora. By all accounts it wasn't a particularly effective disguise. Charles was tall and took long manly strides with his skirts hitched up indecorously high. 'An odd muckle trollop' was one description.

Despite this, the party arrived safely at Rhode Phrionnsa on Skye. There Flora sought the help of Lady Margaret MacDonald of Monkstadt House. Willing, if possibly somewhat taken aback, Margaret gave Flora and Charles provisions so they could carry on their journey. At Portree, Charles bade farewell to Flora, giving her a locket as thanks. He eventually escaped to the continent and lived the rest of his life as an exile. Flora was later arrested and imprisoned in the Tower of London. After acquittal she married and settled on Skye. It was there that she died in 1790. The splendid memorial grave in Kilmuir Cemetery was erected in her honour.

FLORA MACDONALD
PRESERVER OF
PRINCE CHARLES EDWARD STUART

HER NAME
WILL BE MENTIONED IN HISTORY
AND IF COURAGE AND FIDELITY
BE VIRTUES
MENTIONED WITH HONOUR

SOUTH UIST

**Address** Kilmuir Cemetery, Hunglader, IV51 9YU, collide.trainers.intrigues | Getting there
Just off the A 855 with free on-site parking | Hours Accessible 24 hours | Tip Monkstadt
House has been fully restored and is now a restaurant offering Scottish and international
cuisine, as well as luxury holiday accommodation.

# 65 Neist Point
*Not Doris' day*

The Little Minch is the stretch of water between Skye and the islands of Benbecula, North Uist and Harris in the Outer Hebrides. It is not a place to be when the weather is bad, as C. A. Arentz, the captain of the steamship *Doris*, discovered on 12 July, 1909. Owned by the Norwegian firm of Mowinckels Rederi A/S, *Doris* was *en route* to Stettin from Liverpool. Thick fog descended as she was steaming north through the Little Minch. Unaware of the strong currents that flow through the strait, Arentz failed to notice that *Doris* was slowly drifting eastwards. The ship crashed into Neist Point, her engines running at full speed. Arentz ordered his crew and the ship's 13 passengers to abandon ship, and fortunately everyone was saved. Poor *Doris* was stuck fast on the rocks, however, and remained there for two weeks before finally sinking.

Ironically, Neist Point Lighthouse was under construction when the *Doris* was wrecked. The lighthouse was designed by David Alan Stevenson, whose grandfather, father, two uncles, and brother Charles, also built lighthouses around the coast of Scotland. David's daughter, Dorothy, did not become a lighthouse engineer, instead going on to become a best-selling novelist, publishing over 40 books and selling seven million copies. Her cousin, Robert Louis, achieved even greater fame as a writer, with classics such as *Kidnapped*, *Treasure Island* and *The Strange Case of Dr Jekyll and Mr Hyde*.

Neist Point Lighthouse is a handsome structure, not tall but still well proportioned, with a white and buff colour scheme. The light was first lit on 1 November, 1909, just four months after *Doris* met her end, with the foghorn completed on 25 June, 1910. It's a very steep walk down to the lighthouse, and so an aerial ropeway was installed so that supplies could be more easily transported to the crew. Like most lighthouses, Neist Point is now fully automatic and maintained by the Northern Lighthouse board.

Address Waterstein, IV55 8WT | Getting there Take the Waterstein turn-off on the B 884 and park at the Neist Point Car Park (catching.movements.become) | Tip Talisker Bay Beach is a wonderfully secluded cove that looks out onto the Sea of the Hebrides. It's just 20 minutes' drive from Carbost where you can sample whisky at the world-renowned Talisker Distillery.

# 66 Old Man of Storr

*Myths and modern horror*

The Old Man of Storr – *Bodach an Stor* in Gaelic – is one of several jagged rock pinnacles that sit below the fractured cliffs of The Storr, the highest point along the Trotternish Ridge. Legend has it that a race of truculent giants once made Skye their home. One was killed in a fight, and over time his body disappeared beneath layers of earth and rock. Eventually only his thumb remained visible and that is what is now known as the Old Man of Storr. A more mischievous take on the tale is that the Old Man represents an entirely different part of the giant's anatomy altogether… For that reason, the formation was once worshipped by prehistoric Gaelic tribes as a symbol of fertility.

Or perhaps the Old Man had a more romantic origin. Another story describes how a man once saved the life of a brownie, a type of fairy who helped with housework in return for food and shelter. The two became devoted friends. And then one day the man's wife died. His heart broken, the man passed on soon after. Missing his friend, the brownie carved the Old Man of Storr as a loving tribute.

Perhaps these tales are partially why the location is such a draw to the makers of fantasy and horror movies. In the opening credits of *The Wicker Man*, the sweetly innocent police sergeant Neil Howie, played by Edward Woodward, flies over the formation on his way to investigate the disappearance of a child. Although the Old Man is seen only fleetingly, the eerie landscape neatly sets the scene for the terror to come.

The Old Man had a larger starring role in *Prometheus*, the 2012 prequel to *Alien*, directed by Ridley Scott. Set in 2089, the movie follows a team of archaeologists who discover a painted star map in a cave in the face of The Storr. Oblivious to how this sort of thing usually ends, the team blast off into space to find the aliens who created the map. It *really* doesn't go well for them after that…

Address Near Portree, Skye, IV51 9HX, www.isleofskye.com | Getting there Bus 57A to Old Man of Storr Car Park and then a 45-minute walk; just off the A 855 Portree to Uig road with paid parking at the Old Man of Storr Car Park | Tip Kilt Rock, a cliff face on Skye's eastern coastline, is so called because the colour and shape of the basalt columns resembles a pleated tartan kilt. Decide for yourself by viewing the formation from a vertiginous observation point.

# 67 __ Skye Bridge
*Paying a heavy toll*

The 16 October, 1995 was a wet and windy day. A crowd of some 200 watched Steven Campbell, a 10-year-old pupil from Loch Duich primary school, cut a blue ribbon to mark the official opening of the Skye Bridge. Secretary of State, Michael Forsyth, then made a speech before being whisked over the bridge in his chauffeur-driven Rover. Not far away, a more subdued crowd watched as the Skye ferry made its final scheduled journey across Kyle Akin.

A bridge to connect Skye to the mainland was badly needed. Surging visitor numbers meant that the ferries often struggled to cope in the summer months. So there was cause for celebration when a tender to build a bridge was issued by the government in 1989.

The contract was awarded to Miller-Dywidag and funded by the Private Finance Initiative. This meant that Miller-Dywidag would pay for construction of the bridge and in return could charge drivers a toll for using it, which was initially set at £5.20 for cars from May to September, and £4.30 for the rest of the year. Although this was slightly cheaper than the ferry crossing, there were many on Skye who were angry that there were tolls at all.

A pressure group was formed. Skye and Kyle Against Tolls wanted the tolls abolished. Talking to the *Press and Journal*, SKAT member and Highland Councillor Gavin Scott Moncrieff said that 'The bridge is causing a major disruption to the social life of the 10,000 people on Skye and 2,000 people in Kyle', and a John Campbell from Portree described the tolls as 'Skyeway robbery'.

The campaign to remove the tolls continued. Some relief was felt in 1997 when the newly elected Labour government introduced a scheme to subsidise them. And then in 2004, Scottish Transport Minister, Nicol Stephen, announced the happy news that the bridge had been purchased by the Scottish Government and that the collection of tolls would stop with immediate effect.

Address A 87, Kyleakin, IV41 8PG, setting.wheat.reshape | Getting there Free parking at
The Plock in Kyle of Lochalsh | Tip From spring to autumn, a regular ferry service still
connects Skye to the mainland. The MV *Glenachulish* sails daily from Glenelg to Kylerhea
and is the last ferry in the world with a hand-operated full deck turntable.

# 68 Trotternish Ridge

*The ups and downs of a landscape*

The Trotternish Ridge stretches roughly 20 miles in a north-south direction from Portree to a point just west of Flodigarry, where it finally peters out. The ridge includes a number of evocatively named features, such as the Old Man of Storr, the Table, the Needle, the Prison, as well as the mellifluous Quiraing and Bioda Buidhe (or Yellow Peak). It was created by the largest landslide in the British Isles, and one of the largest in Europe.

The rocks that underlie the ridge were formed in the Jurassic period, approximately 165–150 million years ago. This was the heyday of the dinosaurs, when behemoths like Diplodocus strode the Earth, their lives threatened by efficient carnivores such as the truly scary Allosaurus. The rock is sedimentary – a series of layers of sandstone, limestone and shale – laid down gradually over a vast span of time by a warm and shallow sea.

Sixty million years ago, events on Skye took a more dramatic turn. The formation of the North Atlantic and the drift westwards of what is now North America and Greenland resulted in very intense volcanic activity. Molten lava flowed across the landscape from huge fissures, creating a vast plateau of basalt that covered the older Jurassic rock. Ten million years after this, the Trotternish area of Skye began to tilt upwards, creating a series of faults that ran in a north-south direction. This is no coincedence.

The sheer weight of the volcanic rock began to take its toll on the weaker Jurassic formations. Gradually – and sometimes not so gradually – the sedimentary rock fractured and slipped downwards, taking huge blocks of basalt along for the ride. It was this process that created the steep east-facing scarp slopes so characteristic of the Trotternish Ridge. Although Trotternish is now largely stable, the northern end of the ridge is still slowly moving. If you ever find the Flodigarry road closed for repair, this may well be the reason why.

Address Quiraing Road, IV51 9LB, argued.pronouns.defenders | Getting there Bus 57 from
Portree to Loch Langaig footpath; the Trotternish Ridge is a very challenging walk with
no path for much of its length; a good view of the Quiraing and Bioda Buidhe can be had
from the viewpoint near the Quiraing Car Park (fee payable) | Tip If you're ready for a good
hearty feed after a day in the hills, then The Hungry Gull in Staffin is the place for you. Sit
in if you want to rest your feet or get something to go from their takeaway menu.

# 69 Aberfoyle

*Scotland's 'worst' poet waxes lyrical*

Douglas Adams' *The Hitchhiker's Guide to the Galaxy* is a wholly remarkable book. For one thing, the novel helpfully ranks the very worst poets ever. They are (in increasing order of awfulness): the Vogons, the Azgoths of Kria, and Paula Nancy Millstone Jennings of Greenbridge, Essex, England. Strangely, one name that doesn't make the list is that of William Topaz McGonagall, who is often said to be the worst poet in the history of the English language.

McGonagall was born to Irish parents in 1825 or 1830, possibly in Edinburgh, though also possibly somewhere in Ireland (the history of McGonagall's early life is oddly imprecise at times). He was apprenticed as a handloom weaver in Dundee, where, in 1846, he married Jean King, whom he met working in the same mill. McGonagall was a keen reader and a great admirer of Shakespeare, whom he praised in 'An Address to Shakespeare' with the lines 'Immortal! Bard of Avon, your writings are divine / And will live in the memories of your admirers until the end of time'.

According to his autobiography, it was in June 1877 that he 'was seized with a strong desire to write poetry'. Undeterred by rejection by Queen Victoria, he did just that. During his life McGonagall penned over 200 poems, the most famous of which is the (truly dreadful) 'The Tay Bridge Disaster' of 1880. Inspired by Scotland's beauty, he also paid tribute to the otherwise blameless Highland town of Aberfoyle in 'Beautiful Aberfoyle': 'But no words can describe the beautiful scenery / Aberfoyle must be visited in order to see / So that the mind may apprehend its beauties around / Which will charm the hearts of the visitors I'll be bound'. Despite his unique approach to rhyme, McGonagall has undeniably achieved immortality. His fame has grown since his death in 1902, and his work is now appreciated by people all over the world. Could you say the same for many other (better) poets of the time?

Address Stirling, FK8 3UQ, www.aberfoyle.co.uk | Getting there Bus M4 and X10A to Queens Crescent; take the A821 to Aberfoyle and park at Riverside Car Park | Tip The most scenic (and time-consuming) route to Aberfoyle from the A84 is along the A821/Duke's Pass. The highlights on the route are Loch Venachar and Loch Achray, and Tigh Mor, a wonderfully romantic 19th-century hotel where Queen Victoria once stayed.

# 70 Bracklinn Falls
*Great Scott!*

Bracklinn Falls are not the highest or widest or most remote of Scotland's many waterfalls. They are utterly charming, however, particularly in the autumn months when the surrounding woodland is at its golden best. The falls are a series of mini waterfalls created by a succession of natural stone steps, framed by a deep gorge. They are arguably the most dramatic feature on Keltie Water, a river that snakes its way through the Brackland Glen before flowing into the River Teith south of Callander. Bracklinn Falls are also notable for straddling the Highlands Boundary Fault, the geological line that separates the lowland and highland areas of Scotland.

Bracklinn Falls have long been a tourist hotspot. One early visitor was artist J. M. W. Turner, who dashed off a pencil sketch of the falls (with a figure for scale) on a visit to Callander in 1834. Queen Victoria popped by in 1870, a visit for which a cast-iron bridge was built over the gorge. This replaced a bridge roughly three feet wide that consisted of two logs, covered in branches and overlaid with turf. This rustic crossing had been used by local farmers for years, but was obviously thought unsuitable for the Queen.

This was sensible. On 8 October, 1844, *The Sun* reported that newly married Thomas Jamieson visited the falls with his new wife, and sister Elizabeth. A James Taylor found the group at the bridge, which Elizabeth was reluctant to cross. Taylor 'seized her in mere wantonness to place her on the giddy pathway'. Unfortunately, Elizabeth 'fixed her hold upon the railing, which give way'. Both 'were precipitated into the abyss below' and killed.

On a happier note, Bracklinn Falls stirred the imagination of Sir Walter Scott during a stay at the nearby estate of Cambusmore. Scott was working on his poem 'The Lady of the Lake'. In Canto II, Roderick Dhu, the outlawed chief of Clan Alpine, is described as being brave but 'as wild as Bracklinn's thundering wave'.

**Address** Callander, Stirling, FK17 8EN, www.lochlomond-trossachs.org, bottled.wolves.bulky | Getting there Free parking at the Bracklinn Falls Car Park just off Bracklinn Road in Callander, and then a 20-minute walk | Tip As the name suggests, The Old Bank Coffee House and Restaurant has found a home in a former bank, built in the 1870s. Fortunately, you don't have to be a bank manager to afford the available treats from the extensive menu.

# 71 Earthquake House

*Shake it all about*

There are places in the world where earthquakes are common. These are typically places that straddle the boundaries between the Earth's tectonic plates. There are roughly 15 such plates and they move continuously: pulling apart, pushing together, or sliding past each other. We don't feel this movement because they move incredibly slowly – generally only about half an inch a year (roughly the speed that toenails grow). An odd exception to this rule is the Australian plate, which is shifting Australia northwards at a giddy two and a half inches annually – so quickly that co-ordinates for the continent need to be regularly updated to keep mapping data accurate.

Thanks to friction, tectonic plate movement can slow or even stop. This creates stresses that build up over time. It's the sudden release of this stress that causes an earthquake. Sometimes the resulting tremors are barely noticed. Alas, sometimes earthquakes can be absolutely catastrophic. The worst so far this century – at least in terms of lives lost – was the earthquake that hit Haiti in 2010. An estimated 220,000–316,000 people were killed, and buildings in Port-au-Prince – Haiti's capital – were badly damaged.

Britain, you'll be pleased to know, is nowhere near a tectonic plate boundary. However, hundreds of small earthquakes are recorded in Britain every year. Why this should be is something of a mystery. One possibility may be regional compression of the tectonic plate on which Britain sits. What's more puzzling is that eastern Scotland and Ireland are largely free of earthquakes. Comrie in Perthshire is known as 'shaky town' for the simple reason that it's earthquake-prone. So much so that in 1840 the very first seismometer was built in the town by a local postmaster and shoemaker. The small but sturdy building in which it was placed – the Earthquake House – has the unique distinction of being the first purpose-built earthquake observatory in the world.

Address Comrie, Perthshire, PH6 2JU, sheepish.dumplings.fruitcake | Getting there Bus 15, 115 or 890 to Bridge of Ross and then a short walk; take the Dalronnoch turn-off and park in the lay-by near Earthquake House | Hours Viewable from the outside only | Tip The Dunmoid Stone Circle in Comrie is a small but wonderfully atmospheric monument. There is some debate about who had the circle built; it may be Celtic, Saxon or even Roman in origin.

# 72 The Falls of Dochart

*Water sight*

Dorothy Wordsworth was unimpressed by the landscape of Glen Dochart. A journal entry for 5 September, 1803 notes that 'The face of the country not very interesting, though not unpleasing, reminding us of some of the vales of the north of England, though meagre, nipped-up, or shrivelled compared with them'. She was, however, more taken by the Falls of Dochart, and described how 'the river took up a roaring voice, beating its way over a rocky descent among large black stones: islands in the middle turning the stream this way and that; the whole course of the river very wide'.

You don't have to be the sibling of a famous Romantic poet to appreciate the Falls of Dochart, for they are truly spectacular. When in full spate, the foaming waters of the River Dochart tumble noisily over jagged rocks and around the island of Inchbuie. A dry spell can reduce the falls to a disappointing trickle, however.

The best place from which to view the falls is on a wide shelf of rock on the southern bank of the River Dochart. Look north-east from there and you can see the falls, the Bridge of Dochart, and the village of Killin framed by the lofty Breadalbane Hills (Breadalbane or *Bràghaid Albainn* means the 'high country of Scotland').

The Bridge of Dochart was built in 1760 and modified in 1831. Unusually for a relatively short structure, the bridge has seven spans of four main arches and three culverts. It now carries the A 827 and is therefore frequently crossed by traffic. In the early 1930s there were proposals to build a new, more modern road bridge alongside. This idea was thankfully dropped for financial reasons.

Steps from the bridge lead down onto the island of Inchbuie (*Innis Bhuidhe* or 'yellow island'). Inchbuie is the traditional burial ground of the Clan Macnab. The clan clashed with Robert the Bruce at the Battle of Dalrigh in 1306, and lost their lands for a time after Bruce was victorious at Bannockburn in 1314.

Address Gray Street, Killin, FK21 8SL | Getting there Bus 890, C 60 or S 60 to Manse Road; paid parking at Manse Road Car Park just off the A 827 | Tip Killin (or Kinnell) Stone Circle is a prehistoric monument consisting of six upright slabs of grey schist, and was probably constructed in the Neolithic or Bronze Age.

# 73  Lake of Menteith
*The one and only?*

How many lakes are there in Scotland? The answer is: it depends. There are more than 31,400 sizeable bodies of fresh water in Scotland, but they are referred to either as loch – as in Loch Ness – or as lochan, a small loch. There is in fact only one lake in Scotland: the Lake of Menteith near Aberfoyle.

Or is it? There are actually seven other 'lakes' in Scotland. These can be dismissed, however, as they were all created artificially; the Lake of Menteith is all natural, with no added flavours or preservatives. That said, the Lake of Menteith is also known as Loch Inchmahome (or *Loch Innis Mo Cholmaig* in Gaelic), so perhaps it's only half a lake, or half a loch, depending on your preference. Just to muddy the waters even more, as it were, the beautiful 1654 edition of the *Blaeu Atlas of Scotland* has the Lake of Menteith down as 'Loch Inche mahumo'. The atlas was created for Dutch cartographer Joan Blaeu by Timothy Pont, a native Scot who 'traversed widely every region of Scotland, more curiously observed details by eye, and reduced them to some maps'. Should we therefore bow to Mr Pont's knowledge and expertise and stop using the name 'Lake of Menteith' in favour of its more Scottish alternative? And just why *is* it known as a lake anyway?

How the first question is answered is entirely up to you.

To answer the second question, we need to travel back in time to 1238 and the founding of Inchmahome Priory, the ruins of which can be seen on the island at the middle of the lake (loch). The priory was the work of Walter Comyn, Lord of Badenoch, who built it for an order of Augustinian monks from Italy. The priory had a number of important visitors in its day, including a young Mary Queen of Scots. More relevant to our story is that the monks apparently couldn't pronounce 'loch' but could pronounce 'lake'. So the monks get the blame for the anglicised name.

Address Port of Menteith, Stirling, FK8 3RA, stones.shaves.octagonal | Getting there Free parking at the Lake of Menteith Car Park just off the B 8034 (marzipan.playroom.table) | Tip Fancy taking a tank for a spin? You can at the Tank Drive Challenge, where an ex-British Army tank can be yours to control around a custom-built course in an abandoned quarry.

# 74 Loch Katrine

*A lady and an engineer*

In May 1810, Sir Walter Scott put Loch Katrine on the map when his pseudo-historical narrative poem 'The Lady of the Lake' was first published. In the first canto, a huntsman, exhausted from a long day chasing a stag through the Trossachs forest, comes upon Loch Katrine. Scott describes how the loch 'In all her length far winding lay/With promontory, creek, and bay/And islands that, empurpled bright/Floated amid the livelier light'.

'The Lady of the Lake' was an immediate critical hit. A long and detailed contemporary appraisal by George Ellis for *The Quarterly Review* concluded that 'Mr. Scott… may fairly claim a place amongst the greatest masters of his art'. The poem was a commercial success too, selling 25,000 copies in eight months, and for the next century was required reading for school children. 'The Lady of the Lake' is also credited with inspiring a more romantic view of the Scottish Highlands, and helped to dispel the dark cloud that had hung over the region since the Jacobite risings.

Although Victorians avidly read 'The Lady of the Lake', they were more than willing to put Loch Katrine to practical use too. The ever-increasing population of 19th-century Glasgow required a clean and reliable supply of water. A report in 1852 by civil engineer John Frederick Bateman recommended channelling water from Loch Katrine to the city. Despite opposition by private water companies, an Act of Parliament was passed in 1855 authorising work to begin on Bateman's scheme.

The work required the damming of Loch Katrine, the building of a 26-mile-long aqueduct and the construction of a new reservoir at Mugdock. Over 13 miles of tunnels were also dug through bedrock, and four miles of iron pipes were laid. The project was successfully completed in 1859. Loch Katrine now provides over 50 million gallons of water *every* day to the city.

Address Trossachs Pier, FK17 8HZ, seat.genius.blame or Stronachlachar, FK8 3TY, scraper.trespass.upward | Getting there Paid parking at both Trossachs Pier and Stronachlachar | Tip By far the most stylish way to explore Loch Katrine is on the steamship *Sir Walter Scott*, built in 1899 in Dumbarton.

# 75 Loch Lomond
*Who's at fault here?*

Loch Lomond is special in a number of ways. It is the largest body of fresh water by surface area in the British mainland, and the second largest by volume after Loch Ness. Drive up the A 82 from Glasgow to Crianlarich and Loch Lomond will be your constant companion for a good chunk of the journey, often hidden from view but undeniably *there*.

The loch was formed during the last Ice Age by a glacier that ground its way south from the area around Ben Lui, the eroded rocks and debris dumped near Balloch. What Lomond means is a slight mystery. One possibility is that the word is derived from *leamhan*, Gaelic for elm. Or it may have its origins in *laom*, or beacon. This makes more sense when applied to Ben Lomond, a Munro on the eastern side of the loch. So it may be that the loch is named after the mountain, rather than vice versa.

'The Bonnie Banks o' Loch Lomond' is a traditional lament that has its origins in the Jacobite rising of 1745. The lines 'O ye'll tak' the high road, and I'll tak' the low road / And I'll be in Scotland afore ye' probably refers to the noble (and ultimate) sacrifice of a Jacobite in support of his exiled king. The low road is a metaphor for death, rather than a useful route through the Highlands.

The Highland Boundary Fault crosses over Loch Lomond. As the name suggests, it marks the point where lowland Scotland ends and the Highlands begin (hooray!). The boundary stretches diagonally across Scotland, from the Isle of Arran up to Stonehaven in Aberdeenshire. The Highland Boundary is a geological fault line caused by the slow collision of two small continents some 430 million years ago. The collision created a huge mountain range, with peaks that may have been as high as those in the Himalayas today. These mountains were gradually whittled away over the millennia. What remains are the Highlands that we know and love today.

Address Firkin Point, just off the A82, Arrochar, G83 7DL, www.lochlomond-trossachs.org, situates.desks.inferior | Getting there Free parking at Firkin Point | Tip Go underwater and see sharks, rays and turtles, as well as creatures found in the Lochs of Scotland, at SEA LIFE Loch Lomond.

# 76 McCaig's Tower
*Flumgummery?*

A folly is an often-whimsical building or structure that serves no real purpose other than amusement or as a decorative conversation piece. There was a craze for building follies in Britain during the 18th and 19th centuries, when rich landowners built them to add a quirky point of interest to their country estates. McCaig's Tower in Oban has all the hallmarks of a folly, and is sometimes referred to as such by tourists. It's aesthetically pleasing for one thing, resembling nothing less than the Colosseum in Rome in shape if not size. It's also not particularly useful, other than as a place to have a wee wander round and to admire the view from. However, it's not so much a folly as something left sadly uncompleted.

The tower was commissioned and designed in 1895 by John Stuart McCaig, who was a wealthy Oban banker and something of an amateur art critic. McCaig seems to have had two reasons to want the tower built. The first was to erect a permanent monument to his family: a plan featuring statues of his parents, siblings and himself within the structure was made, but never carried out. The second (and more noble) reason was to provide work for local stonemasons during the long Scottish winter months.

McCaig also planned to erect a central museum and art gallery. It remained on the drawing board as McCaig died in 1902. What you see today is essentially what was complete at the time of his death. McCaig did leave thousands of pounds in his will to pay for work to continue on his tower. However, his sister Catherine contested this. A subsequent Court of Session came to the conclusion that McCaig was 'possessed of an inordinate vanity as regards himself and his relatives, so extreme as to amount almost to a moral disease, though quite consistent with sanity'. Catherine won her case. After her death in 1913, the inheritance was used to create an educational endowment now known as the McCaig Trust.

**Address** Duncraggan Road, Oban, PA34 5DP, www.explore-oban.com | **Getting there** Bus 1, 005, 401, 403 or 918 or various others to Oban North Pier Ferry Terminal and then a short (though steep) walk; train to Oban and then an 11-minute walk; take the A 816 to Oban and park at McCaig's Tower Car Park (shrimps.crust.scarecrow) | **Hours** Accessible 24 hours | **Tip** Oban has a long and rich history as a port town. Learn more about Oban at the Oban War & Peace Museum.

# 77 _ Pulpit Hill
*Look down on Oban*

There are two ways to get to the top of Pulpit Hill. If you need (or would even enjoy!) some useful exercise, then follow the signposted path from Albany Street. It's a climb of 239 feet and – depending on your level of fitness – shouldn't take *too* long. However, if that sounds like hard work, then drive to the summit up Crannag a' Mhinisteir. You'll be glad you made the effort whichever method you choose: the view is simply wonderful.

The name Pulpit Hill is connected to the large cube-shaped stone found on the eastern side of the viewpoint. This is known as the Minister's Stone, and was used by ministers who would stand on top to give alfresco sermons to their congregation. At least, that's the theory. Whether this is true or not is curiously undecided.

Face north-east and you look across the bay towards Oban. Dominating the foreground is the Caledonian MacBrayne (CalMac) Ferry Terminal, the busiest of all CalMac's ports. There is a regular service from Oban to a number of Scotland's islands, including Coll, Colonsay, Lismore, and South Uist in the Outer Hebrides – Oban is known as the 'Gateway to the Isles' for good reason. CalMac started as David Hutcheson & Co. in 1851, connecting Glasgow to Oban by steamship via the Crinan Canal, and Oban to Inverness along the Caledonian Canal.

Oban's bay is sheltered by the proximity of the island of Kerrera, which is easily seen from Pulpit Hill (you really can't miss it, it's that close). The island is essentially a huge sheep farm, with only 50 or so permanent inhabitants. Visitors can't take their cars onto the island, so you either walk once you get there, or take your bike and cycle. This does make it a wonderfully tranquil place to spend a day, and increases the chance of seeing interesting wildlife. CalMac operate a regular ferry service to Kerrera, which sails from a small slipway on Gallanach Road.

Address Pulpit Hill Viewpoint, Oban, PA34 4NA, www.explore-oban.com | Getting there Bus 417 and then a short (though steep) walk; limited free parking at Pulpit Hill Viewpoint Car Park | Hours Accessible 24 hours | Tip The Dog Stone on Ganavan Road is a giant, freestanding column of rock. Local legend has it that the giant Fingal left Bran, his faithful dog, tied to the stone while he went off hunting on the Hebrides.

# 78 __ Rob Roy's Grave
*Loveable rogue*

Once upon a time, the MacGregor clan owned Glenstrae, Glen Lochy and Glen Orchy. Unfortunately, they had powerful and well-connected rivals in the Campbells, their neighbours to the south. By the end of the 16th century the Campbells had forced the MacGregors off their ancestral lands. This drove the dispossessed clan to take up cattle raiding to eke out a living. In 1604, King James VI (James I of England) sided with the Campbells and made it a crime to use the MacGregor name. Many took new surnames. Some ignored the ruling and were hanged for their temerity.

It was into this world that Robert 'Rob Roy' MacGregor was born near Loch Katrine in 1671 (he acquired the name 'Roy' in childhood due to his curly red hair). Rob Roy made a good living by running a protection scheme, charging farmers for looking after their cattle and retrieving them if they were stolen. The money he made was used to feed members of his clan and his tenant farmers. Rob Roy was a renowned cattleman too, with a herd of his own. Trouble erupted in 1711 when he borrowed a substantial sum of money from James Graham, 1st Duke of Montrose, to buy more cattle. The man Rob Roy entrusted with the money (a MacDonald) vanished, and so Rob Roy defaulted on the loan. He was declared an outlaw and Graham seized control of his lands. Like his ancestors, Rob Roy took to raiding cattle, targeting Graham's herds in particular.

Rob Roy fought on the side of the Jacobites in the 1715 rising, and was badly wounded at the Battle of Glen Shiel. Under an amnesty in 1725 he submitted to General George Wade, the commander of the British force in Scotland. Rob Roy died on 28 December, 1734, at the respectable age of 63. He was buried at Balquhidder next to his wife Mary, the words *MacGREGOR DESPITE THEM* added to the gravestone. Since then, he has become a folk hero, the subject of numerous books, poems and films.

ROBERT MACGREGOR.
('ROB ROY.)
DIED 28. DEC. 1734. (O.S.)
AGED ABOUT 70.

MACGREGOR DESPITE THEM

**Address** Balquhidder Parish Church, Balquhidder, FK19 8PA, laws.respected.larger |
Getting there Bus 978, C 60 or S 60 to Mhor 84 motel and then a 45-minute walk along a
single-track road; take the turn-off for Balquhidder on the A 84 and park at Balquhidder
Parish Church | Tip Rob Roy's grave lies next to the ruins of Balquhidder Old Kirk, which
was built in 1631 and was long the burial place of the chiefs of the Clan MacLaren.

# 79 __ St Conan's Kirk
## Something for everyone

You could be forgiven for thinking that the architect who designed St Conan's Kirk was somewhat indecisive. The cloister archway is Gothic in style, though the doorway into the church is Norman. The interior styling was heavily influenced by the Kirk of the Holy Isle on Iona, except where it wasn't. The vibrant stained-glass windows are Victorian, though the austere window in the Bruce Chapel was rescued from the 15th-century Church of St Mary in Leith. The Bruce Chapel also features a late 19th-century effigy of Robert the Bruce and a fragment of one of the king's metatarsal bones.

The exterior is similarly eclectic. The 'Saxon' Monkwearmouth Tower is a nod to St Peter's Church in Jarrow on Tyneside, where the Venerable Bede once worshipped. The neighbouring Picard Tower, however, pays homage to a church in France destroyed during World War I. Elsewhere on the exterior you can find humorous representations of owls, hares and a hound, as well as St Conan himself, who whiles away his time looking out across Loch Awe.

St Conan's is the second church built on the site. The first (and plainer) building was completed in 1886 at the instigation of Walter Douglas Campbell. Local legend has it that it was built to save Campbell's elderly mother from a long carriage ride to church. Campbell, who was a younger brother of the 1st Lord Blythswood, was an architect and something of a cultural magpie. During his life, he collected ships' timbers, as well as the windows and royal foot bone mentioned above. Campbell was also a keen student of local legends, as well as being very knowledgeable about architectural style. In 1907, 10 years after his mother's death, he began work on the current church. The eccentricity of its styling is largely Campbell's, though his sister Helen oversaw construction after his death in April 1914. The wonderfully eclectic church is now expertly looked after by the St Conan's Kirk Trust.

**Address** Loch Awe, Dalmally, PA33 1AQ, www.stconanskirk.org.uk | Getting there
Bus 975, 976 or 977 to St Conan's Road Junction; park at St Conan's Kirk just off the A85;
train to Loch Awe | Hours Daily Apr–Sep 9am–6pm; Oct–Mar 9am–5pm (St Conan's
Kirk closes to the public for irregular events, so see website for details) | Tip Nearby
Kilchurn Castle is a ruin now but was once the home of the Campbells of Glenorchy. The
best view of the castle is on the southern side of Loch Awe, with the slopes of Monadh
Driseig looming behind it.

# 80 Ardvreck Castle
*Royalist loyalist*

The jagged ruins of Ardvreck Castle stand on the eastern shore of Loch Assynt. It was built in the 15th century, and was the ancestral home of the MacLeods of Assynt. The castle is notorious as the location for the handing over of James Graham, 1st Marquess of Montrose, a supporter of the Stuart monarchy, to a Covenanter army by Neil MacLeod, the Laird of Assynt.

The Stuarts were not short on self-belief. They believed they ruled Scotland (and from 1603, England too) as a Divine Right, granted by God. This meant that they also considered themselves the spiritual heads of the Church of Scotland. Not everyone held this view, however. In 1638, many in Scotland signed the National Covenant. This opposed any interference in the Church of Scotland by the then Stuart monarch, Charles I. Those who signed the agreement are now known as Covenanters. Naturally, Charles did not look on this favourably. However, in trying to get his way, he made a number of errors that ultimately led to the English Civil War.

By 1650, Charles was dead, executed for high treason 'by the severing of his head from his body'. On the orders of the future Charles II, Montrose had raised an army of German and Scandinavian mercenaries, as well as men from Orkney. On 27 April, Montrose and his army faced a Covenanter force led by Colonel Archibald Strachan at Carbisdale. It did not go well for Montrose. By the end of the day 400 royalist soldiers were dead, and 450 captured, for the (alleged) loss of a single Covenanter.

Accompanied by two supporters, Montrose fled to friendly territory. Unfortunately for him, he crossed land controlled by MacLeod. The young laird captured Graham and had him confined in the castle cellar. It is said that MacLeod was paid 25,000 Scottish pounds to hand over Montrose. The hapless marquess was executed on 21 May, 1650 at the Mercat Cross in Edinburgh.

Address Near Inchnadamph, IV27 4HL, limo.honestly.envoy | Getting there Bus 3A or 809 to Ardvreck Castle; free parking just off the A 837 near the castle | Hours Accessible 24 hours | Tip Ardvreck Castle Waterfall is just a short walk from the A 837. Though relatively small compared with other waterfalls in the area, it's in a picturesque location nestled in a clump of silver birch trees.

# 81 Balnakeil Craft Village

*Waste not, want not*

On 24 April, 1964, a story in the impressively named *Stornaway Gazette & West Coast Advertiser* began with 'A very interesting and very significant development is taking place in Sutherland from which we in the Hebrides could learn a lot'. The piece went on to relate that 'A craft village is being established in Balnakeil, Durness, in an old Air Ministry Site'. The intention was 'to attract experienced craftsmen and talented young people by offering buildings at a very low rental for use as living quarters, studios and workshops'. Wonderfully, this is exactly what happened.

The 'Air Ministry Site' mentioned in the *Gazette* is a collection of buildings erected in the mid 1950s. They were built to house the staff of a proposed MoD early warning station on Faraid Point. The buildings are all single storey and flat roofed, and largely made of concrete. They look a lot like bunkers and wouldn't have been anyone's idea of a comfy home-from-home. Not that anyone ever lived in them. The station was never built, possibly because faster Soviet missiles meant that an 'early warning' from Sutherland would come far too late for the rest of the country.

The site was abandoned and left to rot. It was saved by Hugh Powell, head of industrial design at Leeds College of Art, who, in the company of two officials from Sutherland County Council, visited Balnakeil in 1963. It was Powell who had the idea of turning the site into a communal 'village' for artists. The council bought the site from the MoD and adverts were placed in newspapers to find suitable tenants. The rent for one building (with no electricity or running water) was initially set at £5 a year. The first tenant was Hector Riddell, a silversmith from Tariff in Aberdeenshire. Today, there is a delightfully varied range of artists and businesses who ply their trade at Balnakeil. Pay a visit and you may even be tempted to give up the nine-to-five job and make your home there too.

Address Balnakeil, Durness, IV27 4PT, www.balnakeilcraftvillage.weebly.com | Getting there Bus 805 or 806 to Balnakeil Craft Village; take the Balnakeil Craft Village turn-off on the A 838 and park on-site | Hours The various galleries open at different times so see website for full details | Tip Durness Golf Club boasts the most northerly golf course in mainland Britain.

# 82 Bone Caves
## Ancient animals

On 15 February, 1927, the *Edinburgh Evening News* reported on a meeting of the Society of Antiquaries of Scotland at the National Museum of Antiquities. Under the headline 'Early Man', the article announced 'An important discovery belonging to the old Stone Age in Scotland'. James Cree, when investigating the Inchnadamph district ('a remote and wild area' the piece solemnly notes) had, in 1925, 'discovered in an undisturbed cave part of an antler of a young reindeer and an incisor tooth of a bear, animals long since extinct in Britain'.

The cave in question is one of four in close proximity high up on Creag nan Uamh (fittingly, Gaelic for 'Crag of Caves'). Cree, with colleagues James Ritchie and John Graham Callander, were following up on the work of Ben Peach and John Horne, who had excavated one of the caves in 1889. In the course of their digging, Peach and Horne discovered the bones of Arctic animals in the cave (subsequently named the 'Bone Cave'). Remarkably, no one followed up on this discovery until the expedition of 1925.

Cree returned to Creag nan Uamh in the summers of 1926 and 1927 to fully excavate three of the caves. Over those two years, Cree discovered more animal bones, as well as a portion of a broad iron blade and a human femur. In one of the caves, Cree found the remains of 'vast numbers of shed antler of young reindeer, mostly broken, representing over four hundred individual deer'.

What Cree couldn't do at the time was definitively date the human remains. In the preliminary report prepared for the Society of Antiquaries, Cree, Ritchie and Callander suggested that the bones were Upper Palaeolithic (or more than 12,000 years old) during a time between ice ages known as an interglacial. Carbon dating has since proved that the bones are Neolithic and are (only!) 4,500 years old, which is still a *very* long time ago.

Address Allt nan Uamh, near Inchnadamph, IV27 4HF, ribcage.twigs.descended | Getting there Free parking just off the A 837 at Allt nan Uamh, and then a 40-minute walk along a well-trodden path that's steep on the final climb up to Creag nan Uamh | Tip The bones and artefacts excavated by Cree and his colleagues are now in the National Museum of Scotland in Edinburgh.

# 83__Cape Wrath
## *Turning a corner*

It takes effort to reach Cape Wrath at the north-west corner of Scotland. There is no railway station or airport nearby, and you can't drive yourself there. To start the journey, you first catch a passenger ferry at Keoldale. After zipping across the Kyle of Durness you then disembark onto a tiny concrete jetty. (Note: If you look vaguely competent you may be asked to tie the boat up first.)

You're not at Cape Wrath yet though. You then hop onto a waiting minibus, courtesy of Stuart Ross and his company Visit Cape Wrath. The journey takes roughly 50 minutes, at a stately 10 miles per hour. Despite this slow speed, it's a teeth-rattling trip. The single-track road is rutted and potholed and long overdue for repair, which is unlikely to be any time soon given how few vehicles use the route. Along the way, the driver will point out interesting geological features. This is a wild and remote place known as the Parph, which bears the scars of many a winter storm: wind speeds of 140mph have been recorded. Large areas of the Parph are used as a training area for British and NATO armed forces, though not when the minibus runs, you'll be pleased to note.

Your first sight of Cape Wrath is likely to be the lighthouse that overlooks the cape. The 66-foot structure was constructed in 1828 by Robert Stevenson, a prolific builder of lighthouses and grandfather to the writer Robert Louis Stevenson. The name Cape Wrath derives from the Norse word *hvarf* for a turning point. This is evidence that the Vikings probably used Cape Wrath as a landmark when navigating around the coast of Britain.

Look directly north from the cape and all that stands between you and the Arctic (or Canada if you look due west) is the Atlantic Ocean. You won't have long to take advantage of this unique opportunity though. After an hour it's time to get back on the bus for the bumpy journey back to the ferry and civilisation.

Address Keoldale, Lairg, IV27 4QF, +44 (0)7534 591124, www.visitcapewrath.com |
Getting there Take the A 838; parking at Keoldale and then a short walk to East Keoldale
Pier | Hours The Kyle of Durness ferry and Cape Wrath bus run from May to September,
with trip times determined by the weather and the tides (see website for details) | Tip Have
a bite to eat at the Ozone Café at Cape Wrath. Run by John and Angie, this has to be one
of the most remote cafés in Scotland!

# 84 Clachtoll Beach
*Layers of history*

Sutherland isn't short of wonderful beaches. Clachtoll Beach is no exception, though it's oddly overlooked by holidaymakers in favour of the – admittedly larger – beach at Achmelvich, a near neighbour. However, Clachtoll has a number of interesting attractions lacking at Achmelvich, particularly if you're in the mood for a spot of (careful) exploration and intellectual stimulation.

The first of these is Split Rock, which is easily found on a small headland at the southern end of the beach. The split was probably caused by a section of cliff slipping down an inclined bed of sandstone. Look carefully at the rock and you might be lucky enough to spot curious, thin, rust-coloured bands of… something. The 'something' are microbially induced sedimentary structures, thankfully shortened by scientists to MISS. These are the fossilised remains of microbes that once formed into slimy sheets known as biofilms. This is more exciting than it sounds. Clachtoll's MISS are the oldest fossils in the British Isles, laid down one billion years ago during the Proterozoic Eon. At this point in Earth's history there were no plants or animals. All you'd see (if you somehow found yourself back that far in time) would be lots of very simple, tiny organisms just quietly getting on with the business of existing.

Far, far less old is Clachtoll Broch, found by walking a short distance north from the beach. This ruined Iron Age home was excavated by Historic Assynt in 2017. Evidence showed that the broch was abandoned after a fire broke out and destroyed the timbers in the structure, as well as the thatched roof. Although this was a tragedy for the family, the ash from the fire helped to preserve a fascinating array of domestic artefacts. These included pottery, stone tools, and worked antlers and animal bones. Perhaps the most interesting artefacts were the bone tools used to make woven cloth and to prepare hides to create leather.

**Address** Clachtoll, IV27 4JD, contained.resort.relay | **Getting there** Bus 809 to Beach Road End and then a short walk; take the Stoer turn-off on the B 869 and then park at Clachtoll Beach Car Park (fee payable) | **Tip** If you like a good pie, then Lochinver Larder is the place to head to after visiting Clachtoll. You can even have their pies sent anywhere in Britain.

# 85 __ Croick Church
*Shaming signatures*

The remote Croick Church is a small and rather plain structure, one of 30 in the Scottish Highlands designed by Thomas Telford. It was built in 1827, though it is the church's connection to the Clearances less than 20 years later for which it is truly notable.

In the early 1840s, most of the people living on the Glencalvie estate were tenant farmers, their wives and children. These were men and women whose families had worked the land for generations, making Glencalvie their ancestral home. The estate was owned by the Robertsons of Kindeace, and run for them by James Gillander. It was Gillander who, in 1842, first attempted to evict the tenants in order to more profitably graze sheep on the land. However, it wasn't until 24 May, 1845, that he finally succeeded. Eighteen families – 92 people in total – were forced from their homes.

Carrying whatever possessions they could manage, 80 of them made their way to Croick Church. There they took shelter under a makeshift tent in the churchyard. A reporter for *The Times* was there to see the sorry scene, and described how 'A fire was kindled in the churchyard, round which the poor children clustered; two cradles with infants in them were placed close to the fire, and sheltered round by the dejected-looking mothers.'

A poignant and permanent record of that day can be seen on the eastern windows of the church. There, some of the newly dispossessed scratched names and messages onto the glass. A 'John Ross shepherd' made his mark, as did 'Amy Ross' and a 'C. Chalmers'. One person wrote 'Glen Calvie people, the wicked generation', perhaps believing that this was divine retribution for an undisclosed sin. Within a week the families had moved on, never to return to Glencalvie. Ironically, Gillander was later buried in the churchyard. It's said that for years afterwards his grave was covered with stones and rubbish by those protesting against his cruel actions.

Address Ardgay, IV24 3BS, www.croickchurch.com, fairly.optimists.backpacks | Getting there Parking opposite the church | Hours Viewable from the outside only | Tip Go for a walk or take time to look for Scottish wildlife at the Alladale Wilderness Reserve.

# 86 Dornoch Cathedral

*A saint and a material girl*

Upon election to the Bishopric of Caithness in 1222, Gilbert de Moravia made a very sensible decision. Two of his predecessors had been brutally murdered at Halkirk, the original seat of the diocese of Caithness. So Gilbert understandably moved the seat to the (presumably safer) town of Dornoch. To show willing, he even paid to have a splendid new cathedral built there. Gilbert was by all accounts a good man; he established hospices for the poor, helped to civilise his diocese, and, as legend has it, bested a dragon that was up to no good in the county. Gilbert died in 1245 and was rightly buried in his church. He is now known as St Gilbert – though he was probably never formally canonised – and was the last Scot allotted a place in the Calendar of the Saints.

Dornoch Cathedral has had something of a chequered history. In 1570, it had the misfortune of being badly damaged by fire when a feud broke out between the Murrays of Dornoch and the Mackays of Strathnaver; the roof fell in and only the chancel and transept walls were left standing. Perhaps more shockingly, Gilbert's tomb was desecrated. The cathedral was partly repaired in 1616 by Sir Robert Gordon of Gordonstoun. It wasn't until 1837, however, that the building was restored to its former glory, thanks to the munificence of Elizabeth, Duchess-Countess of Sutherland.

Countless children have been christened in Dornoch Cathedral. However, no bairn has ever received as much attention as Rocco John Ritchie, who was baptised there on 21 December, 2000. The wee chap was the child of pop superstar Madonna and director Guy Ritchie. In the congregation were carefully selected A-list celebrities. Outside, a cohort of journalists and photographers were on station to cover the occasion. According to *The Guardian*, 'the paparazzi flashes were more than a little disconcerting'. Madonna and Ritchie were married at nearby Skibo Castle the following day.

Address Dornoch, IV25 3SH, www.dornoch-cathedral.com | Getting there Bus 25A, X25 or X99 to Clydesdale Bank and then a short walk; take the A949 turn-off on the A9 and then park at Meadows Park Road Car Park | Hours Open during daylight hours except during services | Tip If you've got a sweet tooth then you need to make time to visit Cocoa Mountain in Dornoch.

# 87__Dunrobin Castle
### *Home from home*

There's no missing Dunrobin Castle, perched as it is on a high cliff overlooking Sutherland's east coast. The castle is the largest great house in the northern Highlands and boasts 189 rooms. It has been the continuous seat of the various Thanes, Earls and later Dukes of Sutherland since the 13th century.

The first castle was probably built on the site around 1235, when the Earldom of Sutherland was created. This castle was probably a simple, square but heavily fortified keep, with walls six feet deep. The keep was essentially (and very thoroughly) encased by external additions in the 16th century, and then a large extension was added in 1785. The French-influenced and charmingly elegant structure of today dates to 1845, when the noted architect Sir Charles Barry was commissioned to extensively remodel the castle in the Scottish Baronial style. Remarkably, the original keep is still in there somewhere, which is why Dunrobin is said to be the oldest occupied house in Scotland. Barry also designed the grounds, which he modelled on the gardens at Versailles.

There have been a good number of notable visitors to Dunrobin over the centuries. Queen Victoria and Princess Beatrice stayed there in September 1872, the same month as Sir Henry Rawlinson, President of the Geographical Society, and journalist Henry Morton Stanley. The latter is famous for finding explorer David Livingstone in 1871 near Lake Tanganyika, greeting him with the words 'Dr Livingstone, I presume?', though this is now disputed.

Another visitor was Prime Minister Ramsay Macdonald, who stayed as a guest of the Duke and Duchess of Sutherland in October 1932. According to a contemporary story in *The Irish Times*, the PM's visit to Dunrobin Castle 'was purely for health reasons and had nothing to do with politics', and 'the premier expressed himself as highly satisfied with his visit'. You will be too.

Address Golspie, KW10 6SF, +44 (0)1408 633177, www.dunrobincastle.co.uk | Getting there Bus 906, X25 or X99 to Dunrobin Station; train to Dunrobin Castle; take the Dunrobin Castle turn-off on the A9 and park in the main car park | Hours Daily Apr & Oct 10.30am–4.30pm, May–Sep 10am–5pm | Tip The witch stone in Dornoch marks the site where Janet Horne was executed in 1722. She was the last person to be killed for the crime of witchcraft in the British Isles.

# 88 Hermit's Castle

## *Downsizing*

There's a property in Achmelvich that's ideal if you want to get away from it all. It's a castle, so you can pretend to be the local laird during your stay. It's also *very* close to the sea, so you'll fall asleep to the gentle sound of waves washing against the rocks. There are lots of windows to admire the view from too. And, if that's not enough to convince you, it's also just a hop, a skip and a jump to two pristine bays with the whitest sand you're ever likely to see.

It sounds too good to be true, doesn't it?

Admittedly, there are one or two downsides to Hermit's Castle, as it's known locally. It's thought to be Europe's smallest castle; step across the threshold and you may need to stoop. There's no door to open or close and no glass in the windows, so it's a bit draughty too. There is a fireplace but don't think about making a fire as the chimney is a solid lump of concrete. In fact, everything is concrete, including the shelves and the (single) bed.

As you may have guessed already, this isn't an actual castle. It was the wonderfully eccentric creation of David Scott, an architect from the decidedly non-Scottish town of Norwich. It was built in the early 1950s and took Scott some six months to erect single-handed. According to locals interviewed in the 1980s for *The Scots Magazine*, Scott loved this particular corner of Scotland. He 'expressed a desire to build a retreat in keeping with the mood of the coast and mountains' and the Hermit's Castle was the delightful result. Scott used the castle as a bothy on his visits to Achmelvich for a number of years afterwards, usually after spending the day walking along the coast or painting.

Scott wasn't unsociable. And he definitely *wasn't* a hermit. He was friendly and kept in touch with the locals for several years after his last visit. Eventually, however, the letters stopped coming. What happened to Scott after this is now a mystery.

**Address** Achmelvich, IV27 4JB, searched.public.timer | **Getting there** Bus 809 to Youth Hostel and then a short walk; take the Achmelvich turn-off on the B 869 and then park at Achmelvich Beach Car Park (fee payable) | **Hours** Accessible 24 hours | **Tip** The white sand and turquoise-green waters of Achmelvich Beach are positively tropical so it's not surprising that in summer it's a popular spot for holiday makers. Get there early to bag your place in the sun.

# 89__Kylesku Bridge
*Better by design*

Civil engineering projects in Scotland had a banner year in 1985. Four of the eight awards issued that year by the Concrete Society were won by schemes in Scotland. The overall winner was the Kylesku Bridge. It was deemed by the judges 'as an elegant solution to an intricate problem, which has been achieved in a manner sympathetic to an exceptionally beautiful landscape'. It was also judged remarkable that 'in such a remote location the high standard of finish should have been achieved in conditions which undoubtedly were difficult for reasons of climate and exposure'.

The judges were right. The Kylesku Bridge – officially known by its Gaelic name of Drochaid a' Chaolais Chumhaing – is remarkable. It is 906 feet long and curves in a gently flowing arc over Loch a' Chàirn Bhàin, carrying the A 894 80 feet above the loch. The view from the bridge is splendid too. To the east is Loch Glendhu and the Glendhu Forest, and Loch Glencoul. Dominating the skyline to the south-west is Quinag, a distinctive three-peaked mountain range; two of the peaks – Sàil Gharbh and Sàil Ghorm – can be seen from the bridge.

Work on building the bridge commenced in the summer of 1982. The contract was awarded to Morrison Construction and Lehane, Mackenzie and Shand, who beat four other firms for the job. On 8 August, 1984, the bridge was opened by Queen Elizabeth II, accompanied by Princess Margaret. It was a grey and wet day. Clad in a raincoat and sheltered under an umbrella, the Queen cut a tartan ribbon to conclude the ceremony.

The new bridge saw the end of the 200-year-old Kylesku ferry service (which was originally just a rowing boat used by crofters taking cattle to market, their cows swimming alongside). Ferryman Jim McQuillan told the Queen that the bridge would make five men redundant, but admitted that it was 'a sign of progress'.

Address Kylesku, IV27 4HW, believer.magpie.professes | Getting there Free parking in car parks just off the A 894 on either side of the bridge | Tip Take a boat tour around Glencoul and Gledhu sea loch with Kylesku Boat Tours. Along the way you'll see Eas a' Chual Aluinn, Britain's highest waterfall with a sheer drop of 660 feet.

# 90__ The Old Man of Stoer
*Climbing to the top*

The Old Man of Stoer is a 200-foot-tall sea stack off the western coast of Sutherland. It was first climbed in June 1966 by Tom Patey, Brian 'Killer' Henderson, Brian Robertson and Paul Nunn. Patey later described the climb in a technical but wonderfully down-to-earth article for the May 1967 edition of the *Scottish Mountaineering Club Journal*. In the opening paragraph he dismisses an earlier description of the Old Man of Stoer as 'evidently quite unclimbable' with the short but thoroughly emphatic 'He is not'.

To climb the Old Man, the four borrowed ladders from George, the owner of a local hotel. To reach their destination, the climbers first had to descend the mainland cliff. This was 'quite difficult' according to Patey, as to save time they 'scrambled down a 200-foot fixed rope with the ladders balanced awkwardly round our necks. The penalty of a slip was instant decapitation'. The ladders were used to bridge the wave-lashed gap between the mainland rocks and the base of the Old Man. Despite this ingenuity, thanks to the weight of his equipment, Robertson got wet: 'By the time he had slid down to the half-way mark his rucksack was submerged and the water lapped about his ears.' After this adventure, the climb was challenging but safely concluded, although a nesting fulmar did drench Patey and Robertson in 'foul-smelling slime'. Since then, the Old Man of Stoer has been a popular destination for climbers wishing to emulate the feat. There are now a number of recognised routes to the top, of varying degrees of difficulty.

Sadly, both Paul Nunn and Tom Patey were killed in later climbing adventures. Nunn died in August 1995 when he and fellow climber Geoff Tier were buried by an ice-fall in the Karakoram range in Asia. Patey lost his life on 25 May, 1970 while abseiling down The Maiden, a sea stack on the north Sutherland coast. A bronze cross was later placed at the summit in his honour.

**Address** Near Raffin, IV27 4JG, rubble.noun.delays | **Getting there** Free parking at Stoer Lighthouse Car Park (cascade.insurance.intend) off the B 869 and then a one-hour walk | **Tip** The sandy and sheltered Clashnessie Bay beach is a great place for kids to play and adults to explore.

# 91 RAF Memorial
*Mountain tragedy*

The Avro Anson was a British twin-engined monoplane designed in the mid-1930s, initially for coastal maritime reconnaissance. Although an unglamorous aircraft, it was reliable and popular with aircrews, who nicknamed it 'Faithful Annie'. During the war the Anson was primarily used as an aircrew trainer, a role it kept until the type was withdrawn from service in 1968.

A memorial at Inchnadamph Old Kirk pays tribute to six RAF aircrew who lost their lives flying an Anson on 13 April, 1941. The crew were from 19 Operational Training Unit and were flying Anson N9857 out of RAF Kinloss on the Moray Firth. They were on a cross-country training flight to Oban. From there the crew would navigate to Stornaway on the Isle of Lewis, before returning to Kinloss via Cape Wrath and Achnashellach Station.

The pilot was Flying Office James Steyn. Also on board were Pilot Officer William Drew as the flight's Observer (Navigator); Sergeant Charles Mitchell was an Observer under training; Flight Sergeant Thomas Kenny was a Wireless Operator / Air Gunner; and there as Wireless Operators / Air Gunners under training were Sergeant Jack Emery and Sergeant Harold Tompsett.

The cloud base that day was low and Steyn had to fly below 500 feet. The weather worsened as the flight progressed. The runway at RAF Stornaway was closed due to snow and so Steyn headed back to Kinloss through the Highland mountains. A final radio message from Kenny reported that the plane was icing up. Despite Steyn's best efforts, the aircraft crashed into Beinn an Fhuarain near Inchnadamph. It wasn't until 25 May, 1941 that the Anson was found by a local shepherd. At least three of the crew are thought to have survived the accident but later succumbed to exposure on the bleak mountain. The six were buried side-by-side near their aircraft. They remain there still, a rocky cairn marking the spot.

ROYAL AIR
FORCE
FLYING OFFICER
J. H. STEYN, DFC
PILOT OFFICER
W. E. DREW
FLIGHT SERGEANT
T. B. KENNY
SERGEANT
J. EMERY
C. M. MITCHELL
H. A. TOMPSETT

HERE ARE COMMEMORATED
THE CREW OF AN AIRCRAFT
CRASHED ON BEN MORE
ON THE 13TH APRIL 1941
WHOSE BODIES
REST WHERE THEY FELL

Address Inchnadamph Old Kirk, Inchnadamph, IV27 4HL, trap.tinned.gratitude | Getting there Just off the A 830 with limited free parking next to the church | Tip Inchnadamph Old Kirk has been turned into a small but perfectly formed museum. Inside you can see a series of interpretation panels that thoroughly tell the story of the area.

# 92__ Smoo Cave
## *Rock of Ages*

There are three different types of rock: igneous, sedimentary and metamorphic. Igneous rock is formed when molten rock, such as lava or magma, cools and solidifies. Granite is a type of igneous rock, as is basalt. As the name suggests, sedimentary rock is formed from sediments, either sand or mud, or from the remains of animals or plants, which are compacted and cemented together at the bottom of rivers or shallow seas. Sedimentary rocks, such as limestone, are very prone to erosion, something that we'll come back to in the next paragraph. Finally, metamorphic rocks are rocks that have been altered in some way below ground, either by pressure or heat. Lewisian Gneiss, found along the western Sutherland coast, is metamorphic, and is the oldest rock in the British Isles.

Another Scottish geological record breaker is Smoo Cave, a sea cave on the northern Sutherland coast near Durness. At 49 feet high and 130 feet wide, the entrance is the largest entry into a sea cave in Britain. It is also the only cave in Britain formed by the actions of both saltwater and freshwater. Smoo Cave is in a limestone cliff formed roughly 461–526 million years ago. The large outer chamber was created by the relentless whittling effect of the sea over the millennia. Now, however, except at particularly high spring tides, the sea rarely reaches the entrance of the cave. (The term spring tide refers not to the season, but to the higher-than-average tides that occur when the moon is either full or new.)

The two inner chambers were shaped by rainwater and the freshwater stream that still flows out of the cave. Over time, the water slowly dissolved the carbonate dolomites that form the limestone. At times of wet weather, water cascades down a blow hole into the cave as an impressive waterfall. A wooden walkway makes it easy to see the first of the inner chambers. During the summer months you can book a boat tour to explore the second.

Address Durness, IV27 4QA, www.smoocavetours.com, readers.anguished.fetching |
Getting there Bus 803 to Smoo Cave; just off the A838 with limited free parking at Smoo
Cave Car Park or paid parking at Smoo Cave Pay and Display Car Park | Tip The Sango
Sands Viewpoint is a wooden boardwalk that leads to fantastic views across Durness Bay
and Durness Beach.

# 93 The Split Stane

*Old Nick nicks old rock*

The ancient boundary between Caithness and Sutherland is marked by The Split Stane, a neatly cleaved boulder on the side of a road near the hamlet of Melvich. There is of course a perfectly rational explanation for the geological oddity, one that probably involves frost damage or erosion. However, a legend told locally is far more fun. The story unfolds something like this…

It is a dark and moonless night. A young woman is walking home to Melvich from the village of Reay. As the woman makes her way across the lonely moor, she senses that someone is following closely behind. Fearing for her life, she starts to run as fast as she can. Daring to glance behind, the woman sees that it is the Devil himself who is in hot pursuit. Finally, her breath ragged from the flight, she reaches the safety of the boundary stone. With a gasp of effort, she leaps over the rock and into Sutherland. Frustrated that he is unable to catch the woman, the Devil stops and curses diabolically. Maliciously he slices the stone in two with his tail, before vanishing in an acrid cloud of yellow sulphurous smoke.

Another local tale involving the Devil captures him in a more magnanimous mood. In Halkirk, the Horseman's Word was used by horsemen to gain total control over their steeds. However, only the Devil could pass on the secret word, and only on receipt of a living creature as settlement for services rendered. The crafty horsemen would ensure that this was always an otherwise useless cockerel, carefully kept hidden under an upturned basket until payment was due. And then one day a boy filled with curiosity lifted just such a basket, setting the cockerel free and trapping himself underneath. When the Devil raised the basket to claim his prize, the horseman was horrified at the sight. He immediately called for the parish minister to intercede. After much haggling by the minister, the Devil relented and swapped the child for the cockerel.

Address On the A836, approximately two and a half miles east of Melvich,
wakes.configure.cassettes | Getting there Free parking at the Mackay Country Landmark
Car Park and then a 20-minute walk along the A836 | Tip Melvich Beach is a wonderfully
secluded and quiet sandy bay just a few minutes' walk from Melvich.

# 94__ Suilven

*Star quality*

Climbing a mountain is a useful metaphor for life. It's a journey for one thing, with a very definite beginning and end. Reaching the top will be difficult, requiring courage and fortitude to overcome whatever hardships the mountain throws your way. You need to be well prepared too, planning your route beforehand and not just winging it on the day. Also, it's hard on the knees.

Climbing mountains is a popular theme in movies. We know what a character will have to go through to reach the top, and eagerly follow their progress step by painful step. When they reach the top we rejoice. And that joy is all the sweeter if the character has overcome a personal flaw or disadvantage.

The eponymous protagonist in *Edie* is in her eighties, an age when most people have hung up their hiking boots. Played by Sheila Hancock, Edie has had a disappointing life. Widowed, she faces the prospect of spending her final years in a home. What spurs Edie to change her life is the discovery of an old postcard of Suilven, sent by her father. This reminds her of the happy life she had before marrying her joyless and controlling husband. Edie travels to Inverness where she is accidentally knocked over by Jonny and his fiancée, Fiona. She reluctantly accepts help from Jonny, who drives her to Lochinver from where she plans to climb Suilven. After a lot of self-doubt and physical pain, Edie makes it to the top. The film ends with Edie and Jonny standing on the summit, their triumphant smiling faces aglow in the light of the setting sun.

What's even more inspiring is that Sheila Hancock actually climbed Suilven to film the role. In an interview for the movie, Hancock said that it was 'tough, but kind of wonderful to be doing that at my age', and that 'it's a huge change for old people to see someone portraying age as lively and exciting'. Which, if not quite a metaphor, is exactly the way it should be.

**Address** Near Lochinver, cherished.theme.improving | **Getting there** Unfortunately, there's no convenient road that gets you directly to the base of Suilven. One route starts on the Canisp Road (presume.shred.prosper). Another starts from a car park in Inverkirkaig (feuds.mandolin.comments). Whatever the route, the walking is hard and long and so shouldn't be considered lightly | **Tip** Other charismatic mountains nearby include Stac Pollaidh on the Coigach Peninsula and Ben More Assynt, the highest peak in Sutherland.

# 95 ___ The Wee Hoose

*Lo-res des-res*

The Wee Hoose sits on a small island at the southern end of Loch Shin. It is well named, for it truly is wee, unless it's just further away than you think… The man who built the Wee Hoose was a Jock Broon, who, in 1824, was given the island by a local duke in gratitude for sharing the secret of distilling whisky.

As locals tell it, the island was far bigger before that date, but Broon had to fell a lot of trees to clear a space to build his hoose. Sadly, Broon later died after shooting himself in the foot while poaching deer. The hoose was inherited by Broon's elder son, Joseph, who, following in Jock's footsteps, distilled whisky on the island. Joseph, known locally as Joe, died in 1929, having married five times, sired 9 children and welcomed 54 grandchildren into the world. This complicated family history led to the hoose standing empty until the will could be untangled. It has been in the care of Joe's descendants ever since, most of whom still live there.

Except… If you regularly read *The Sunday Post* (and if not, why not?) you'll be rightly suspicious of the story. Jock and Joe Broon are both characters in the long-running comic strip 'The Broons', printed each week in the newspaper. Jock 'Paw' and Maggie 'Maw' Broon look after their children, the grown-up Joe, Hen, Daphne and Maggie, and pre-adolescent Horace, the curiously never-named Twins (though one may be called Eck), and The Bairn, or wee lamb. And not forgetting Grandpaw Broon, who pops in regularly to share his homespun view of life or get up to mischief.

Even more suspicious is the fact that a strangely similar house to the Wee Hoose was built in the late 1990s and paraded on a float during the Lairg Gala. So which is it? An unlikely tale of whisky-distilling dukes? Or something lovingly put together for a day of celebration that was too good to throw away afterwards? Go see the Wee Hoose and decide for yourself.

**Address** Lairg, IV27 4AZ, ordering.skyrocket.vessel | **Getting there** Bus 2, 4, 805 or 806 to War Memorial and then a short walk; free parking on the A 836 and then a short walk | **Hours** Viewable from the shoreline of Loch Shin only | **Tip** The Falls of Shin can be found in ancient woodland. If you're lucky, you'll see salmon leap the falls on their way to their spawning ground.

# 96 Ardnamurchan Point
*Westward Ho!*

If you think about it, mainland Britain is a truly odd thing. It's weirdly non-regular in shape and bits of it jut out untidily with no concession to sense or practicality. The geography can also be something of a puzzle. A significant fraction of England is further north than a good chunk of Scotland, for instance. And that's not the only confusing cardinal conundrum. Land's End in Cornwall is the most westerly point in Britain, right? It really should be; the Cornish peninsula sticks a long way out into the Atlantic. And yet, inexplicably, it isn't. The most westerly tip of mainland Britain happens to be the largely unknown Ardnamurchan Point in Lochaber.

Actually, that's not entirely true. The most westerly point of mainland Britain is Corrachadh Mòr, just under a mile south of Ardnamurchan. However, Corrachadh Mòr isn't *that* much further west and it's a strenuous walk over rough and rocky ground to get there; you can drive to and park at Ardnamurchan Point, which is undeniably far more convenient.

Another reason to stick with Ardnamurchan Point is its austere yet handsome lighthouse. It was designed by Alan Stevenson and completed in 1849. Uniquely, it was built in an Egyptian style. This is readily apparent in the detailing around the entrance to the tower, in the decorative corbels below the light, and in the design of the chimney stacks of the keeper's cottage.

Alan Stevenson was one of a distinguished family of lighthouse designers and engineers. His father, Robert, designed the lighthouses at Cape Wrath and Dunnet Head, as well as others around the Scottish coast. Alan's brothers, David and Thomas, also built lighthouses, the latter successfully experimenting with electric light in 1869. Thomas' son, Robert Louis, failed to follow the family tradition, however, preferring (fortunately for the history of literature) to write novels instead.

Address Kilchoan, PH36 4LN, puppets.terribly.attaching | Getting there Take the
Lighthouse turn-off on the B 8007 and park at Ardnamurchan Lighthouse | Tip After the
long drive to Ardnamurchan Point you'll probably be ready for a cup of tea and a sandwich.
From April to October, both of these – and more! – can be had at the Stables Coffee Shop
at Ardnamurchan Point.

# 97 __ Ben Nevis
## *'You take the high road'*

Looming over Fort William, Ben Nevis is the highest mountain in Britain. The Scottish Highlands, you won't be surprised to learn, dominates Britain's 'highest mountains' list. Snowdon (or more properly, Yr Wyddfa), the loftiest peak in Wales, is 19th on the list. The first 18 are all in Scotland. At least Snowdon makes the top 20; Carrauntoohil in Ireland is the 31st highest mountain in the British Isles, England's Scafell Pike languishes at a relatively lowly 46th, and poor Slieve Donard in Northern Ireland is 81st.

Despite its stature, Ben Nevis is easily accessible thanks to its proximity to Fort William; there's no need to spend days trekking to base camp, or even spend a night under canvas before making a final push for the summit. Ben Nevis is no cakewalk, however. Since 1849 there have been over 100 recorded fatalities on the mountain. People have been killed in avalanches, or fallen down steep edges or over cliffs. The summit is often covered in cloud, and the weather can change for the worse in a matter of minutes. In 2023, analysts for Holidu, a German holiday company, declared Ben Nevis to be the second most dangerous natural wonder in the world, beaten only by the considerably higher Mont Blanc; the conclusion was reached by comparing the number of annual visitors to a place with the average number of deaths per year.

Perhaps the strangest ascent of Ben Nevis was that made by Henry Alexander Jr. Henry and his team drove a modified Model T Ford to the top in order to prove that mass-produced cars were just as good as those that were hand-built, as well as to promote his father's car dealership in Edinburgh. The pioneering drive began on 9 May, 1911 from Torlundy near Fort William. On 13 May, Henry arrived at the top. Curiously only the descent was filmed. The footage was long thought lost but was rediscovered in 2015. It can be viewed for free on the British Film Institute's website.

Address Fort William, PH33 6TE, marble.messaging.hacksaw | Getting there The Mountain (or Tourist) Route starts at the Ben Nevis Visitor Centre in Glen Nevis. Despite this being a relatively simple route to follow, it still requires a decent level of fitness, good boots and appropriate clothing. Check the mountain weather forecast before setting out and allow six to nine hours to complete the walk | Tip A bronze sculpture of Henry and his Model T Ford can be seen on Cameron Square in Fort William.

# 98 Buachaille Etive Mòr

*Climb a Munro today*

Ask a child to draw a picture of a mountain and they will probably draw something not unlike Buachaille Etive Mòr. The north-eastern face of Buachaille is delightfully triangular, as all mountains should be. The name is Gaelic for 'the great herdsman of Etive', Etive being the glen below. Buachaille is actually four peaks in total, Stob Dearg (the triangular bit), Stob na Doire, Stob Coire Altruim and Stob na Bròige, arrayed along a ridge five miles in length.

Stob Dearg and Stob na Bròige are both Munros, the name given to Scottish mountains over 3,000 feet. The name refers to Sir Hugh Munro, a Victorian aristocrat from Kirriemuir. Munro was a keen mountaineer, who helped found the Scottish Mountaineering Club in 1889. It was the editor of the SMC's *Journal* who asked Munro to compile a list of every Scottish mountain over the magic figure. This Munro did using Ordnance Survey maps of Scotland, as well as comparing notes with other members of the SMC. His list was first published in the *Journal*, volume 1, no. 6 in September 1893.

Munro initially had 283 mountains on his list. However, the number has fluctuated over the years as more accurate measurements have been made, and mapping data refined. Today, the SMC lists 282 Munros in total and 509 tops (separate subordinate summits on a Munro, such as Stob na Doire).

At 4,411 feet, the highest Munro is of course Ben Nevis. At the other end the scale, Beinn Teallach only just squeaks onto the list at 3,001 feet. Stob Dearg (3,351 feet) is 109th on the list and Stob na Bròige (3,128 feet) is 210th. To climb a Munro is to bag it. The first person to climb every Munro in one continuous round was Hamish Brown, who managed the feat in 1974. Munro himself never bagged every Munro. He died in 1919 of pneumonia, caught while in France running a troop canteen. There were only three peaks on his list that he had yet to climb.

**Address** Ballachulish, PH49 4HX, acid.studio.headrest | Getting there Start from the free car park at Altnafeadh and follow the route past the bothy at Lagangarbh. As with any walking in the hills of the Scottish Highlands, you'll need a decent level of fitness, good boots and appropriate clothing; take note of a mountain weather forecast before setting off, and allow seven to nine hours to complete the walk | Tip Go for a drink or a meal, or spend a night in a comfortable bed at the nearby Kingshouse Hotel.

# 99 Caledonian Canal
*Making a connection*

It's a mere 62 miles between Fort William and Inverness. Hop in a car and you could make the journey in less than two hours, barring roadworks or holiday traffic. Now, try to imagine Britain without motor vehicles and modern roads, or a rail network for that matter. On foot, that same journey would now take days, particularly if you were weighed down with belongings. To make the situation worse, now imagine you have a lot of very heavy goods – several tons say – that you need to transport between the two towns.

One solution would be to load your precious cargo onto a ship (let's make it a sailing ship too, just for fun!). Unfortunately, this now requires a long and potentially dangerous voyage up to and around the top of Scotland. What to do? This was the tortuous problem facing people in the 18th century. The solution was to build a canal through the Great Glen that would connect Fort William and Inverness, via Loch Linnhe and Loch Ness.

Planning work on what would become the Caledonian Canal began in 1773, when the route was first surveyed by engineer James Watt. Exactly 30 years later, an Act of Parliament was passed that authorised the construction of the canal. Civil engineers Thomas Telford and William Jessop were commissioned to survey the route again, and to oversee the building of the canal. The work was expected to take a mere seven years and estimated to cost £474,000 (or roughly £41,000,000 today). Both predictions were incorrect.

The 60-mile-long canal eventually opened in 1822, at a final cost of £910,000. In total there are 29 locks on the route, including Neptune's Staircase, the longest staircase lock in Britain. The canal was immediately useful, and remained so even when the railways spread across the Highlands. Today, the waterway is mainly used by tourists in pleasure boats wanting to see Scotland from a different and less hurried perspective.

Address Thomas Telford Corpach Marina, Corpach, PH33 7JH, www.corpachmarina.co.uk, or Sea Lock House, Inverness, IV3 8RE | Getting there For Corpach take bus 145, 500, 502 and various others to Kilmallie Hall; train to Corpach; take the Corpach turn-off on the A 830 and park at the marina. For Inverness take bus 28, 48A, 307 or 307A to Clachnaharry Inn; take the Mid Street turn-off on the A 862 and park at Sea Loch House | Tip See the 'Secret Portrait' of Bonnie Prince Charlie at the West Highland Museum. This anamorphic painting of Charles can only be seen correctly when viewed as a reflection on a silvered cylinder.

# 100___ Camusdarach Beach
*Texan takeover?*

It's hard to believe that someone once planned to build an oil refinery on the delightfully beautiful Camusdarach Beach. Well, not really. But that was the premise of the 1983 feel-good movie *Local Hero*, written and directed by Bill Forsyth.

'Mac' MacIntyre (Peter Riegert) works for Knox Oil and Gas in Houston, Texas. He is sent to the Scottish Highlands by Felix Happer, the very odd owner of Knox Oil, to negotiate the purchase of the (fictional) village of Ferness and its neighbouring beach. Cleverly, the movie upends expectations. The villagers are *more* than happy to sell out and move on, though they cannily pretend to be indifferent to the prospect to push the purchase price up. Mac meanwhile falls in love with life in Ferness. He increasingly feels uncomfortable with his task and all that would follow should he succeed. Fate intervenes in the form of Ben Knox (Fulton Mackay), who lives in a shack on the beach, which he owns the deeds to. Ben, understandably, doesn't want to sell up, much to the frustration of the villagers and secret delight of Mac. No spoilers here, however. You'll just have to watch the movie if you want to know how this knotty problem is resolved.

*Local Hero* was filmed in a number of places across Scotland. The real village of Pennan in Aberdeenshire stood in for Ferness. Thanks to the magic of the movies, you don't notice that this is on the other side of Scotland to Camusdarach Beach, where Ben's shack scenes were filmed. A scene outside Ferness church was also filmed at Camusdarach. Don't go looking for the church though, as this was constructed purely for the movie and dismantled once filming ended. Other locations in the Highlands to look out for are Loch Tarff – where Mac and his British Knox contact, Danny Oldsen (Peter Capaldi), accidentally injure a rabbit when driving to Ferness – and Moidart near Fort William.

**Address** Near Morar, PH40 4PD, alarming.item.launcher | **Getting there** Take the B 8008 to Camusdarach Beach Car Park (free parking) and then a short walk | **Tip** If you like seafood then The Cabin in Mallaig is a must. There's plenty of choice when it comes to freshly caught shellfish, but the classic fish and chip supper is hard to beat.

# 101 Castle Stalker

## 'Your mother was a hamster'

The islet on which Castle Stalker sits has been owned by a number of families since the early 14th century. The first owners were the Mac-Dougalls, whose clan head was the Lord of Lorn. This title (and ownership of the islet) was passed to the Stewarts in the late 14th century. Castle Stalker was built by Sir John Stewart in the mid-15th century to replace a smaller structure that originally stood there. In 1620, a drunken wager led to the Campbells of Airds taking possession. For the next three centuries, the two families vied for ownership until, in 1908, Charles Stewart bought the islet and the castle back, and it has remained in Stewart hands ever since.

For part of the day, Castle Stalker is protected by the waters of Loch Linnhe. However, Loch Linnhe is a sea loch and is therefore tidal. At low tide, the water recedes and Castle Stalker can be reached on foot along a causeway.

The castle was a key location in 1975's *Monty Python and the Holy Grail*. Shooting the movie tested the patience of the Pythons as the budget was small and the weather often poor. To add to the problems, finding suitable exterior locations proved tricky. Permission to shoot at castles belonging to the National Trust for Scotland was refused as the script was 'not consistent with the dignity of the buildings'. Fortunately, owners of privately owned castles, such as Doune, and of course Castle Stalker, were more amenable.

Castle Stalker stood in for the fictional Castle Aaargh, seen near the end of the film after King Arthur (Graham Chapman) sails to the islet on a magical boat. Unfortunately, he is then repeatedly taunted from the castle battlements by a Frenchman with an outrageous accent (John Cleese). Frustrated by the encounter, Arthur fails to recover the Holy Grail that is hidden within. Rallying his army, he prepares an attack but is arrested by the police before he can do so. The film then comes to an abrupt sto…

Address Just off the A 828 between Ballachulish and Connel, Appin, PA38 4BL, www.castlestalker.com | Getting there Bus 405 to Post Cottage; limited on-street parking nearby | Hours Viewable from the outside only except during pre-booked tours (see website for details) | Tip The Castle Stalker View Café and Giftshop is a family-run business that serves home-made food and offers a wide range of hot and cold drinks, all of which can be enjoyed while looking at splendid views across Loch Linnhe.

# 102   Clachaig Gully
*Because it's there*

Clachaig Gully in Glen Coe is a vertical slash on the flank of Sgòrr nam Fiannaidh. The gully is, according to the Scottish Mountaineering Club, a (very!) steep ascent of 1,706 feet. It was once used by hikers as the route down from Sgòrr nam Fiannaidh, though this is not recommended, as the going is treacherous (the SMC regard it as a 'hair raising descent'). Clachaig Gully is best tackled as a climb, and then only by those with good climbing technique.

The Massacre of Glencoe, also known as *Murt Ghlinnhe Comhann* or the 'Murder of Glencoe', occurred near Clachaig. This brutal event took place on 13 February, 1692, just four years after the exile of the Catholic King James VII of Scotland (James II of England). Many Highland clans still supported James and opposed the new Protestant regime of King William and Queen Mary. The Battle of Killiecrankie of 1689 between Jacobites and government troops was a victory for the rebels, but the revolt quickly fizzled out.

In August 1691, King William offered a pardon to the Jacobites on condition that the clans swore an oath of allegiance to the new monarchs. Failure to do so would invite punishment by 'the utmost extremity of the law'. Clan leaders who had sworn an oath to James were in a quandary until he released them from their obligations on 12 December, 1691, though this news only reached the Highlands three days before the end of the year.

Alasdair MacDonald set off to swear the oath on behalf of his clan. However, machinations by members of the Campbell clan – enemies of the MacDonalds – resulted in his missing the deadline. Government troops under the command of Captain Robert Campbell were billeted with the MacDonalds in Glencoe under the pretext of seeking shelter. Twelve days after arriving, and with no warning given, the troops slaughtered 38 MacDonalds, including Alasdair. Campbells have been scorned in the area ever since.

**Address** Old Village Road, Glencoe, PH49 4HX, itself.free.prefect | **Getting there** Take the Clachaig Inn turn-off on the A 82 and use the (limited) off-road parking on the Old Village Road opposite the Clachaig Inn | **Tip** The Clachaig Inn prominently displays a sign at the entrance declaring *No hawkers or Campbells*. If neither applies to you, inside you'll find a wide range of beers, wines and spirits, as well as a very tempting menu of hearty pub food.

# 103 Commando Memorial
*Special forces*

The two world wars of the 20th century were vastly different in character. World War I was a war of attrition along a largely static front line in northern France. World War II was far more dynamic, with no fixed front line and a greater range of tactics deployed by both sides. One British innovation was the formation of the Commandos, a small force of volunteer soldiers and marines recruited from the army and navy.

The Commando Brigades were trained to perform small but precisely targeted raids in enemy territory. Before D-Day, Commandos were dropped into occupied Europe either by parachute or by landing boat. This was a very risky strategy for the men, as demonstrated during a raid on the Port of Dieppe on 19 August, 1942, named Operation Jubilee. Of the roughly 6,000 soldiers who took part – 1,075 of whom were Commandos – 3,600 were captured, wounded or killed, and much materiel lost.

More successful was Operation Basalt, a raid on the occupied Channel Island of Sark. This led Adolf Hitler to issue his notorious 'Commando Order' on 18 October, 1942. This decreed that 'all men operating against German troops in so-called Commando raids in Europe or in Africa, are to be annihilated to the last man'. This brutal edict applied 'even if these individuals on discovery make obvious their intention of giving themselves up as prisoners'.

Commandos were trained at Achnacarry near Spean Bridge at the Commando Basic Training Centre (CBTC). There the men learnt the skills necessary to survive in hostile territory, including unarmed combat, woodcraft, climbing and demolition. Any soldier who failed the training would be 'returned to unit' and sent back to his original regiment. The Commandos were disbanded at the end of the war. The Commando Memorial, designed by Scott Sutherland, was unveiled by the Queen Mother in 1952.

**Address** Near Spean Bridge, PH34 4EG, bought.wallet.uncouth | **Getting there** Take the Gairlochy turn-off on the A82 and park at the Commando Memorial Car Park | **Tip** Nearby Highbridge is a ruined bridge over the River Spean. It was built by General Wade in 1736 and was the site of the Battle of High Bridge, now seen as the first skirmish in the Jacobite rising of 1745.

# 104 Glen Nevis
## *That's Mamores*

There are many splendid glens in the Scottish Highlands. Which is the most beautiful though? That's a question that's almost impossible to answer. Glen Nevis (*Gleann Nibheis*) would be in with a shout, though, as it truly is wonderfully scenic. It's also conveniently close to the bustling town of Fort William, which is a bonus if you like your natural splendour close to civilisation.

The glen has been used in a number of film productions, including a blink-and-you'll-miss-it appearance in *Monty Python and the Holy Grail*. Glen Nevis was more extensively used as a location in *Rob Roy*, starring Liam Neeson, as well as in Mel Gibson's *Braveheart*; coincidentally at the same time in the summer of 1994. *Rob Roy* is just about the more historically accurate of the two movies, though which is the better film is a fun argument you can have with friends or family. (It's *Rob Roy* in case you were wondering.)

As the name suggests, Glen Nevis is associated with Ben Nevis, the glen curving around the western and southern flanks of the mountain. The most spectacular feature of Glen Nevis has to be Steall Falls (*An Steall Bàn* or 'The White Spout'), which flows into the Water of Nevis. Steall Falls has a 390-foot drop, and is the second highest waterfall in Britain. The highest – Eas a' Chual Aluinn – is happily also in the Scottish Highlands.

On the opposite side of the glen to Ben Nevis are the Mamores, a cluster of 10 Munros and other less lofty peaks. The punningly named Ring of Steall is a 10-mile route that starts at Achriabhach in Glen Nevis and requires the summiting of four of those Munros: An Gearanach, Stob Coire a' Chàirn, Am Bodach and Sgùrr a' Mhaim. The most nerve-racking and vertiginous stretch of the route is the aptly named Devil's Ridge, which is an arête – a sharp mountain ridge – with a steep slope on either side. No one would argue with you if you decide to give it a miss.

Address Fort William, PH33 6SY, disengage.detection.corrosive | Getting there Car or bus N 41 to Youth Hostel; take the Glen Nevis turn-off on Belford Road / North Road roundabout and then park at Braveheart Car Park, Ben Nevis Visitor Centre or Lower Falls Car Park (fee payable at all), or park for free at Steall Waterfall Car Park | Tip The main Braveheart Car Park was built during the filming of the movie. The Braveheart village was constructed further south in Glen Nevis, roughly one mile beyond the Youth Hostel. There is a small, free car park located nearby.

# 105_Glenfinnan Monument
*Clansman*

It wasn't a good time to be a Highlander following the defeat of the Jacobite army at Culloden. The victor, Prince William, Duke of Cumberland and the youngest son of King George II, wasn't a man for forgiveness. Nearly 3,000 Highland troops were captured after the battle. Many died of disease on their way to prison, crammed into the holds of transport ships with their comrades. Despite this, there were far too many men to put on trial for treason. And so, a lottery system was devised. The Highlanders were divided into groups of 20 and made to draw lots. The unfortunate loser stood trial as an example to the rest. If found guilty he would in all likelihood be executed by hanging, drawing and quartering, a truly grisly death.

Life didn't improve in the century that followed. This was the time of the Highland Clearances, when roughly 70,000 Highlanders were evicted (often forcibly) from their homes and farms by landowners and their agents. The justification for this was simple but heartless. Wool was a very profitable commodity during this period. This meant that landowners could make far more money raising sheep than renting out tenant farms. As a result, some Highlanders were forced to scratch a living on marginal coastal land; others ended up in towns and cities such as Glasgow. Many, however, emigrated to North America, never to see their homeland again.

The Glenfinnan Monument commemorates the efforts of the Highlanders at Culloden, and acknowledges the dreadful sacrifice they made. It was built at the instigation of local landowner Alexander Macdonald of Glenaladale, whose father's cousin had supported the Jacobites. The 60-foot-high cylindrical stone column was built in 1815, and the sculpture of the Highlander perched on top was added in the 1830s. It's a fitting and romantic tribute to a people who lost so much in what was ultimately a doomed cause.

**Address** Glenfinnan, Lochaber, PH37 4LT, crowned.kiosk.fingertip | **Getting there** Just off the A 830 with paid parking at the Glenfinnan Viaduct and Monument Car Park | **Tip** The great wizard Albus Dumbledore was buried on Eilean na Moine Island at the western end of Loch Eilt (proudest.scouted.wishing). The grave is first seen in *Harry Potter and the Deathly Hallows – Part One*. You can see the island from the shore of the loch, though the surrounding countryside was altered digitally for the movie.

# 106 Glenfinnan Viaduct
*Full steam ahead*

Is the Glenfinnan Viaduct a towering achievement of late Victorian engineering know-how built to transport a railway line across a wide Highlands valley? Or is it a magical structure found on the route to Hogwarts School of Witchcraft and Wizardry?

The railway line in question is the West Highland Railway, which connects Fort William and Mallaig. Work on the line began in January 1897 under the supervision of Robert McAlpine and Sons, with Simpson and Wilson providing the engineering knowledge. McAlpine was born in 1847 and founded his construction company in 1869 at the very young age of 22. He was widely known as 'Concrete Bob' for his innovative and pioneering use of the material.

It was concrete that was used to build the Glenfinnan Viaduct as the local stone (largely mica-schist, quartz and gneiss) was too hard to work into useful building blocks. According to the detailed, but oddly compelling, 'Some Concrete Viaducts on the West Highland Railway' (1907), 'Even supposing that the requisite number of men to work such stone could have been secured, the cost would have been prohibitive'. The viaduct eventually cost £18,904 to build, the equivalent of £2,002,200 today.

The Glenfinnan Viaduct is 416 feet long and is 100 feet tall at its highest point. Today it is Scotrail whose diesel trains ply their way backwards and forwards along the line and across the viaduct. However, in the summer months West Coast Railways run *The Jacobite* steam locomotive twice a day between Fort William and Mallaig. The sight of *The Jacobite* puffing its way over the viaduct is truly heartwarming. It's little wonder then that movie makers have tapped into this experience. The West Highland Railway is also known as the Hogwarts Express after the Glenfinnan Viaduct was used to thrilling effect in *Harry Potter and the Chamber of Secrets*, the second movie featuring the eponymous student wizard.

Address Glenfinnan, Lochaber, PH37 4LT, showed.obscuring.spike | Getting there Just off the A830 with paid parking at the Glenfinnan Viaduct and Monument Car Park | Tip Take a journey through the history of the Glasgow to Mallaig railway at the Glenfinnan Station Museum.

# 107 The Great Glen

*A true north/south divide*

Look closely at a map of Scotland and you'll notice something odd. Between Fort William and Inverness there looks to be a 62-mile gash running diagonally up the country. It's easy to imagine that one sharp tug on northern Scotland would neatly, if inconveniently, separate it from the south. This striking geographical feature is the Great Glen, also known as Glen Albyn (*Gleann Albainn*) or Glen More (*Gleann Mòr*). Adding to the effect that Scotland could so easily be torn in two is a series of lochs along the length of the Great Glen, of which the largest is Loch Ness.

The Great Glen cuts a usefully natural swathe through the Highlands, and so was the logical route along which to build transport links from north to south. The Caledonian Canal connects the various lochs in the glen to provide a direct water route between the North and Irish seas. Effectively running parallel to the canal, the A 82 provides a similar service for road users. And walkers needn't feel left out either. The Great Glen Way is a largely low-level route that starts next to the ruins of the Old Fort in Fort William and ends 79 miles later at Inverness Castle.

The Great Glen is a strike-slip fault, formed approximately 430–390 million years ago when the Laurentia and Baltic tectonic plates collided (very, very slowly). This was during the late Silurian and early Devonian periods, a time when the earliest fish were making a first bid for glory. The fault doesn't stop at Fort William or Inverness, however. It continues south under the Irish sea to Donegal Bay and north towards Shetland. There is no movement associated with the Great Glen now, though you may feel the occasional mild earthquake. The worst in recent history affected Inverness on 18 September, 1901. According to *Nature*, reporting a week later, 'chimney-stacks, or parts of them fell down' and 'a long crack was formed in the north bank of the Caledonian Canal'.

**Address** Corpach Marina, Corpach, PH33 7JJ or Sea Lock House, Inverness, IV3 8RE |
Getting there Bus 145, 500, 502 and various others to Kilmallie Hall; train to Corpach; just
off the A 830 with free parking at Corpach Marina; bus 28, 48A, 307 or 307A to Inn; free
parking at Sea Loch House | Tip Uncover the world beneath your feet at Treasures of the
Earth. This private collection of gems, crystals and fossils is one of Europe's largest.

# 108 Kinlochleven
*Water features*

The friendly village of Kinlochleven was created in the early 1900s when the hamlets of Kinlochmore and Kinlochbeg were merged. It is, or rather was, a 'company town' where the 700 men and women who worked for the North British Aluminium Company (now Rio Tinto Alcan) made their home.

Construction of a large-scale aluminium smelter in Kinlochleven began in 1905. The site was chosen for the abundance of water flowing down from the surrounding mountains. Converting raw bauxite to alumina requires astonishing amounts of electrical energy. This was provided by a hydroelectric plant created at the same time as the smelter, fed by Blackwater Reservoir four miles to the east. The plant was the largest hydroelectric power station in Britain when it began operating. It generated so much electricity that all the houses in Kinlochleven were also connected to the supply, the first village in the world to achieve this notable feat. Kinlochleven was often referred to as 'the electric village' for this reason.

The smelter closed in June 2000 and the buildings were demolished, although the hydroelectic plant still remains, and now feeds power into the National Grid. The loss of the works could have seen the end of Kinlochleven. However, a report in *The Guardian* in May 2000 noted that 'the community in the electric village is refusing to lie down and die'. Happily, this has proved to be the case. The village thrives, thanks to the hard work of the Kinlochleven Land Development Trust, with tourism driving the recovery. This is largely due to its position as the penultimate stop north on the West Highland Way, new facilities such as The Ice Factor, a popular indoor climbing centre, and the River Leven Brewery, as well as nearby natural wonders like Grey Mare's Tail. The latter is a 160-foot-high waterfall on the Allt Coire na Ba, which drops vertically (and noisily) into a splendid wooded gorge.

**Address** Wades Road, Kinlochleven, PH50 4QT, pothole.besotted.clusters | **Getting there** Bus 144 or N44 to Kearan Road End; take the Wades Road turn-off on the B 863 and park at the Grey Mare's Waterfall Car Park (fee payable) | **Tip** See a different view of Grey Mare's Tail by taking a guided walk across the new Via Ferrata – or Iron Way – recently added above the cliff down which the waterfall cascades.

# 109 __ Monster Midge
*Testy tetse*

They arrive with the coming of summer. Thousands of them, gathering in huge swarms wherever you go, getting in your way and making life thoroughly miserable. There's really no escaping them either. It's tempting to stay at home, pull the duvet over your head and settle down there till autumn and the onset of cooler weather. However, that's enough about tourists. What about the other infamous pest that Scotland is sadly known for? *Culicoides impunctatus*, more commonly known as the Highland midge.

Midges are tiny winged insects, related to house flies and gnats. During the spring and summer months, adult midges feed on blood, obtained by biting their victims – sheep, deer, cattle, and, unfortunately for us, humans. Curiously, it's the female midge that's the real problem; males have an altogether more vegetarian diet. The lively lassies cluster together in dense clouds, attracted by the carbon dioxide exhaled by their quarry. To ensure a good flow of blood, the hungry midge injects an anticoagulant into the bite. It's this that causes the real irritation, often resulting in red itchy lumps on the surface of the skin that can last for hours. Some lucky people are unaffected, which is scant consolation for those who are.

There are a number of solutions to the problem. Midges are more active at either end of the day, so avoiding those times can help. Wearing bright clothing is said to be oddly effective at warding the blighters off. And they don't fly if there's a strong breeze, so picking a windy day for a walk is a sensible strategy. There are also many types of repellent available and, if the problem is particularly bad, there's always the option of wearing a midge net over your face.

One midge it's hard to avoid is the *Monster Midge*, a great lump of granite onto which someone has painted a huge mouth filled with hideous pointed teeth. Fortunately, the *Monster Midge* is too heavy to fly, otherwise it really would be the stuff of nightmares.

Address Near Ardtoe, Acharacle, PH36 4LD, screaming.flaunting.scornful | Getting there Just off the B 8044 with free parking at Ardtoe and then a 10-minute walk | Tip Ardtoe beach is a great place to explore and spend time looking for shells or admiring the view across to the Isle of Eigg.

# 110 Rannoch Moor

*A place to get away from things*

The flat and boggy moorland of Rannoch Moor is said to be the last wilderness in Britain. There are many stories told about the moor, some of which are even true.

The black waters of Loch Ba and Lochan na h-Achlaise are said to be the home of shape-shifting kelpies. On land these mythical creatures take the form of grey or white horses. Anyone foolish enough to mount a kelpie in its horse disguise is doomed to be whisked off into the depths of the lochs to drown. Other strange creatures that inhabit the moor are ghost dogs, the only trace of which are disembodied shadows that follow travellers.

Robert the Bruce used Rannoch Moor as a place of refuge in the summer of 1306. Bruce had been crowned King of Scots at Scone in March that year, much to the annoyance of King Edward I of England. The two monarchs fought at the Battle of Methven in June, a fight that Edward 'Hammer of the Scots' Plantagenet won. Bruce made the sensible tactical decision to hide on Rannoch Moor until he could rally support for a rematch.

Bruce wasn't the only person to use Rannoch Moor as a place to hide. David Balfour and Alan Breck Stewart, the two heroes of Robert Louis Stevenson's novel *Kidnapped*, also find themselves on Rannoch Moor at one point. The pair are making their way to Edinburgh after fleeing the wood of Lettermore following the murder of Colin Roy Campbell, for which both are wrongly accused.

James Bond (Daniel Craig) in the company of M (Judi Dench), head of MI6, drive across Rannoch Moor in the 2012 movie *Skyfall*. The two are heading for Bond's titular ancestral home, where the spy plans to make a stand against the story's villain, Raoul Silva (Javier Bardem). Anyone looking for the remote house on Rannoch Moor will be disappointed. It was built for the movie on Hankley Common in Surrey, and dismantled afterwards.

Address Off the A 82, Bridge of Orchy, PA36 4AG | Getting there Free off-road parking on the A 82 near Lochan na h-Achlaise viewpoint (thudding.basin.stubbed) or at the Loch Ba viewpoint (sides.cluttered.deriving) | Tip Warm up at the Glencoe Mountain Resort Café with a hot drink or meal (or both!) and do so while enjoying the view across to Buachaille Etive Mór.

# 111 The Well of the Seven Heads

*Look around you*

This sorry tale began with two murders. Alexander MacDonald, the 13th chief of the MacDonalds of Keppoch, had returned from schooling in France with his brother Ranald. To celebrate their homecoming, a grand party was held on 25 September, 1663 at the mansion of Insch, near the village of Roybridge.

At some point in the revelry there was a violent scuffle. During the fight, Alexander and Ranald were killed by seven of their cousins, the MacDonalds of Inverlair. Why the two brothers were murdered is a mystery. It's entirely possible that they were mocked for their newly acquired French manners, and so decided to confront their tormentors. However, Alexander was an unpopular figure in the area thanks to his attempts at clan reform. Perhaps his murder was a convenient and permanent way to thwart his ambitions.

Whatever the reason, there were no repercussions for two years. The killers were well known locally and many sympathised with their actions. One person who *did* want justice was Iain Lom, Gaelic Poet Laureate of Scotland and a kinsman. Lom first appealed to Lord Macdonell of Glengarry and Aros, High Chief of the Clan Donald, who refused to help. The same was true of Sir James Macdonald of Sleat. Lom then went to Sir James of Duntulm Castle on Skye. Using all his skills as a bard and poet, Lom told Sir James that 'Abel is cold and his blood is crying in vain for vengeance…'. This did the trick, for Sir James persuaded the Privy Council in Edinburgh to raise men to avenge the murders. Fittingly, it was Lom who led the men to Inverlair, where the murderers were caught and decapitated. It was also Lom who took the severed heads to Lord Macdonnell. On the way, Lom stopped to wash them in Loch Oich. The grisly monument to commemorate this act was raised on the shores of the loch in 1812.

Address A 82, Loch Oich, Spean Bridge, PH34 4EA, escalates.either.drama | Getting there Bus 915, 916 or 919 to Seven Heads Store; parking at Loch Oich Car Park | Tip The well long pre-dates the monument and is reached via steps.

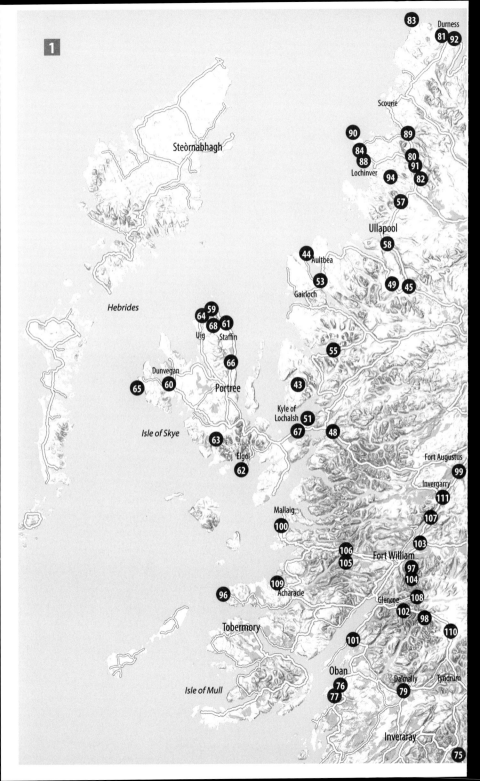

Gillian Tait
**111 Places in Edinburgh**
**That You Shouldn't Miss**
ISBN 978-3-7408-1476-2

Tom Shields, Gillian Tait
**111 Places in Glasgow**
**That You Shouldn't Miss**
ISBN 978-3-7408-2237-8

Gillian Tait
**111 Places in Fife**
**That You Shouldn't Miss**
ISBN 978-3-7408-0597-5

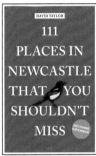

David Taylor
**111 Places in Newcastle**
**That You Shouldn't Miss**
ISBN 978-3-7408-1043-6

David Taylor
**111 Places along Hadrian's Wall**
**That You Shouldn't Miss**
ISBN 978-3-7408-1425-0

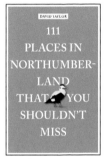

David Taylor
**111 Places in Northumberland**
**That You Shouldn't Miss**
ISBN 978-3-7408-1792-3

Ed Glinert, David Taylor
**111 Places in Yorkshire**
**That You Shouldn't Miss**
ISBN 978-3-7408-1167-9

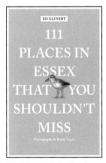

Ed Glinert, Karin Tearle
**111 Places in Essex**
**That You Shouldn't Miss**
ISBN 978-3-7408-1593-6

Ed Glinert, David Taylor
**111 Places in Oxford**
**That You Shouldn't Miss**
ISBN 978-3-7408-1990-3

Lindsay Sutton, David Taylor
**111 Places in Lancaster**
**and Morecambe**
**That You Shouldn't Miss**
ISBN 978-3-7408-1996-5

John Sykes, Birgit Weber
**111 Places in London**
**That You Shouldn't Miss**
ISBN 978-3-7408-2379-5

Alicia Edwards
**111 Places for Kids in London**
**That You Shouldn't Miss**
ISBN 978-3-7408-2196-8

Nicola Perry, Daniel Reiter
**33 Walks in London**
**That You Shouldn't Miss**
978-3-7408-1955-2

Michael Glover, Benedict Flett
**111 Hidden Art**
**Treasures in London**
**That You Shouldn't Miss**
ISBN 978-3-7408-1576-9

Terry Philpot, Karin Tearle
**111 Literary Places in London**
**That You Shouldn't Miss**
ISBN 978-3-7408-1954-5

Solange Berchemin,
Martin Dunford, Karin Tearle
**111 Places in Greenwich**
**That You Shouldn't Miss**
ISBN 978-3-7408-1107-5

Ed Glinert, Marc Zakian
**111 Places in London's East**
**End That You Shouldn't Miss**
ISBN 978-3-7408-0752-8

Jonjo Maudsley, James Riley
**111 Places in Windsor**
**That You Shouldn't Miss**
ISBN 978-3-7408-2009-1

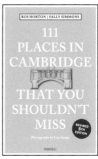

Rosalind Horton,
Sally Simmons, Guy Snape
**111 Places in Cambridge
That You Shouldn't Miss**
ISBN 978-3-7408-1285-0

Phil Lee, Rachel Ghent
**111 Places in Nottingham
That You Shouldn't Miss**
ISBN 978-3-7408-2261-3

Ben Waddington, Janet Hart
**111 Places in Birmingham
That You Shouldn't Miss**
ISBN 978-3-7408-2268-2

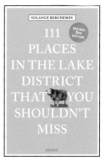

Solange Berchemin
**111 Places in the Lake District
That You Shouldn't Miss**
ISBN 978-3-7408-1861-6

Cath Muldowney
**111 Places in Bradford
That You Shouldn't Miss**
ISBN 978-3-7408-1427-4

Kim Revill, Alesh Compton
**111 Places in Leeds
That You Shouldn't Miss**
ISBN 978-3-7408-0754-2

Michael Glover,
Richard Anderson
**111 Places in Sheffield
That You Shouldn't Miss**
ISBN 978-3-7408-2348-1

Julian Treuherz,
Peter de Figueiredo
**111 Places in Manchester
That You Shouldn't Miss**
ISBN 978-3-7408-2246-0

Julian Treuherz,
Peter de Figueiredo
**111 Places in Liverpool
That You Shouldn't Miss**
ISBN 978-3-7408-1607-0

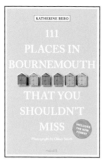

Katherine Bebo, Oliver Smith
**111 Places in Bournemouth**
**That You Shouldn't Miss**
ISBN 978-3-7408-1166-2

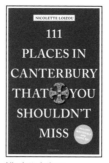

Nicolette Loizou
**111 Places in Canterbury**
**That You Shouldn't Miss**
ISBN 978-3-7408-0899-0

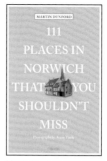

Martin Dunford, Karin Tearle
**111 Places in Norwich**
**That You Shouldn't Miss**
ISBN 978-3-7408-1733-6

Elizabeth Atkin, Laura Atkin
**111 Places in County Durham**
**That You Shouldn't Miss**
ISBN 978-3-7408-1426-7

Martin Booth, Barbara Evripidou
**111 Places in Bristol**
**That You Shouldn't Miss**
ISBN 978-3-7408-2001-5

Martin Booth, Barbara Evripidou
**111 Places for Kids in Bristol**
**That You Shouldn't Miss**
ISBN 978-3-7408-1665-0

Alexandra Loske
**111 Places in Brighton and**
**Lewes That You Shouldn't Miss**
ISBN 978-3-7408-1727-5

Norman Miller, Alexandra Loske
**111 Places in Chichester**
**and West Sussex**
**That You Shouldn't Miss**
ISBN 978-3-7408-1784-8

Catriona Neil, Adrian Spalding
**111 Places in Cornwall**
**That You Shouldn't Miss**
ISBN 978-3-7408-1901-9

Jo-Anne Elikann, Susan Lusk
**111 Places in New York**
**That You Must Not Miss**
ISBN 978-3-7408-2400-6

Floriana Petersen, Steve Werney
**111 Places in San Francisco**
**That You Must Not Miss**
ISBN 978-3-7408-2058-9

Laurel Moglen, Julia Posey,
Ludmila Zotova
**111 Places in Los Angeles**
**That You Must Not Miss**
ISBN 978-3-7408-1889-0

Andrea Seiger, John Dean
**111 Places in Washington, DC**
**That You Must Not Miss**
ISBN 978-3-7408-2399-3

Amy Bizzarri, Susie Inverso
**111 Places in Chicago**
**That You Must Not Miss**
ISBN 978-3-7408-2402-0

Dana DuTerroil, Joni Fincham,
Daniel Jackson
**111 Places in Houston**
**That You Must Not Miss**
ISBN 978-3-7408-2265-1

Cristyle Egitto, Jakob Takos
**111 Places in Palm Beach**
**That You Must Not Miss**
ISBN 978-3-7408-2398-6

Harriet Baskas, Cortney Kelley
**111 Places in Seattle**
**That You Must Not Miss**
ISBN 978-3-7408-2375-7

Susan Veness,
Simon Veness, Kayla Smith
**111 Places in Orlando**
**That You Must Not Miss**
ISBN 978-3-7408-1900-2

## Notes

Most of the places in this book are easily found without too much effort. More obscure places will have three (often very unusual) words follow on after the normal address details. Type these words exactly as shown into the what3words app or website (what3words.com) and they will help you navigate to that place, whether you're getting there on foot, by public transport or in your car.

Mobile phones are great, but a good map, such as those produced by Ordnance Survey, and a compass are preferable in so many ways. There's a lot to be said for going on a mountain navigation course too before heading out into the hills for the first time.

The weather can be changeable in the Highlands, so hope for the best but prepare for the worst. Waterproofs and good walking boots are essential, as is wearing layers that will keep you warm but that can be removed gradually if you get too hot. Always tell someone where you are going, the route you intend to take, and when you expect to return. Have fun but take care, stay safe and live to enjoy the hills on other days.

## Acknowledgements

For their invaluable assistance I'd like to thank Jacky Brookes of the National Trust For Scotland; Hazel Williams at the Braemar Highland Games Centre; Mary Bowers at the Cromarty Courthouse Museum; Lesley Junor at High Life Highland; Donald Henderson and the Wick Society; Scott Clark at Dunrobin Castle; Charlie Ross and Harry Tayler at Wolfburn Distillery; Liz Mackay and the Friends of St Conan's Kirk; Matt MacPherson at The Malt Room; Michelle Anderson and Historic Environment Scotland; Liz Manson at Dornoch Cathedral.

Thank you to Laura Olk at Emons Verlag and Ros Horton of Cambridge Editorial too, for their hard work in getting this book ready for publication. Thank you also to fellow photographer Michael White for his company in the Highlands. And thank you to my wife Tania, for everything.

**David Taylor** is a professional freelance land-scape photographer and writer who lives in Northumberland. His first camera was a Kodak Instamatic. Since then he's used every type of camera imaginable: from bulky 4x5 film cameras to pocket-sized digital compacts. David has written over 40 books, as well as supplying images and articles to both regional and national magazines. When David is not outdoors he can be found at home with his wife and an increasingly large number of tripods.

www.davidtaylorphotography.co.uk

The information in this book was accurate at the time of publication, but it can change at any time. Please confirm the details for the places you're planning to visit before you head out on your adventures.